Hammer on the Rock

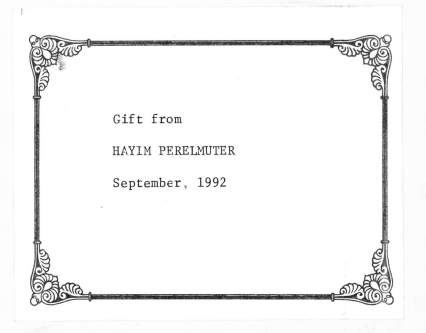

Hammer on the Rock

A SHORT MIDRASH READER

EDITED BY NAHUM N. GLATZER

SCHOCKEN BOOKS · NEW YORK

TRANSLATED BY JACOB SLOAN

First SCHOCKEN PAPERBACK edition 1962
Sixth Printing, 1977

IN CONTRAST to the Bible — the Written Law — the post-biblical tradition was not intended to be handed down in written form. Talmudic Judaism trained up living messengers of its teachings, who took the place of inanimate books and could thus preserve all the immediacy and freshness of their message without its being exposed to that danger of date and dogma which imperils any book.

Even when political and economic crises finally made written compilations necessary, these did not take the form of books, but rather of concise minutes, stenographs almost, of the deliberations on the law carried on in the academies of Palestine and Babylonia. Dialogues, short marginal notes, epigrams and brief passages, page after page betray and preserve the original oral character of the material.

The present book draws its material from the nonlegal parts of the Talmud, the *Haggadah* (or *Aggadah*) and the *midrashic* writings, which originated in the period of the Talmud (the first five centuries C.E.) and which were enriched and expanded in the centuries that followed.

This collection is not intended to take the place of larger compilations. Like the material of which it is composed, it aims to be brief but weighty — to give in a small space some of the more succinct, imaginative, and eloquent examples of talmudic-midrashic thinking and living, each selection being able to suggest a broader vista and a wider range of implication.

The talmudic sages and their followers dressed their utterances in the clothes of scriptural exegesis; even when they gave expression to a new — at times a revolutionary — idea, it was given in the form of a commentary to the eternal word of the Bible. The Holy Scriptures, in their eyes, anticipated, encompassed, and transcended all the possibilities of the future.

The Midrashim being a commentary on the Pentateuch and other books of the Bible (whether in fact or in form only), this reader follows the Pentateuch in its ordering of the material. This naturally makes for a loose arrangement, to which a last chapter treating of the messianic theme is appended.

There is a kind of midrashic literary form, arising out of its original oral character, and partaking, of course, of much of the nature of a dialogue. I have sought to emphasize this midrashic form by breaking up the material, which is normally run together, into individual lines and paragraphs.

In the Notes I have occasionally elucidated a difficult term or pointed out a historical parallel; they have intentionally been kept modest in scope as part of the general purpose of this volume to encourage an appreciation of the texts themselves, from within, and to induce the reader to find the criteria of the meaning of the Midrashim in the Midrashim themselves — for it was in this manner that they were read throughout the ages.   N.N.G.

Hammer on the Rock

"Is not My word like . . . a hammer that breaketh the rock in pieces?" (JER. 23:29). As the hammer splits the rock into many splinters, so will a scriptural verse yield many meanings. — SANHEDRIN 34A.

An Index with explanatory notes
is appended.

I

IN ITS DUE TIME

Rabbi Tanhuma began and said:
"He has made everything beautiful in its time" (Eccles.3:11)
— in its due time was the world created.
The world was not fit to be created before then.
Rabbi Abbahu said:
From this we learn that the Holy One, blessed be he, kept
    creating worlds and desolating them, creating worlds and
    desolating them,
until he created these worlds of heaven and earth.
Then he said: "These please me; those did not please me."

THE GRASSES WENT FORTH

"And the earth brought forth grass, herb yielding seed after
    its kind, and tree bearing fruit, wherein is the seed
    thereof, after its kind; and God saw that it was good"
    (Gen.1:12).

Rav Asi objected:

It is written: "And the earth brought forth grass," on the
second day of the week,

and it is written: "No shrub of the field was yet in the earth"
(Gen.2:5), on the sixth day of the week

— teaching us that the grasses went forth and stood on the
threshold of the earth,

until the first man came and sought compassion in their be-
half, and then the rains fell, and they grew.

HARMONY

You find that the Holy One, blessed be he, created heaven
and earth with wisdom.

Rabbi Azariah said in the name of Resh Lakish:

On the first day He created heaven and earth.

Five days were left: one day he created something on high,
and something below, the next.

He created the firmament on high on the second day; on the
third "Let the waters . . . be gathered together" below.

On the fourth day "Let there be lights" on high; on the fifth
"Let the waters swarm" below.

Only the sixth day was left for something to be created on it.

The Holy One, blessed be he, said:

If I create something on high, the earth will be angry.

If I create something below, heaven will be angry.

What was it the Holy One, blessed be he, did?

He created man from that which is below, and the soul from
that which is on high.

Say: "The Lord by wisdom founded the earth" (Prov.3:19).

"And God said: Let us make man" (Gen.1:26).

Rabbi Simon said:

When the Holy One, blessed be he, came to create the first
    man,

the ministering angels divided into parties and factions,

one saying: Let him not be created,

and another saying: Let him be created.

Mercy saying: Let him be created, for he will be merciful,

and Truth saying: Let him not be created, for he will be all
    lies.

Righteousness saying: Let him be created, for he will do
    righteous deeds,

Peace saying: Let him not be created, for he is all contention.

What did the Holy One, blessed be he, do?

He took Truth and flung him to the earth.

The ministering angels said to the Holy One, blessed be he:

    Master of the universe, do you disgrace your own seal?

Raise Truth from the earth.

Rav Huna said:

While the ministering angels were still arguing and disputing,

the Holy One, blessed be he, created man.

Then He said to them:

Why do you argue? Man is already made.

FROM ALL THE WORLD

It is taught: Rabbi Meir used to say:

The first man, his dust was gathered together from all the
    world.

Rabbi Oshayah said in the name of Rav:
The first man, his body came from Babylon, his head from
   the land of Israel, and his limbs from the other countries.

ONE PILLAR

It is taught: Rabbi Yose says:
Woe to the creatures that see and know not what they see,
stand and know not upon what they stand.
Upon what does the earth stand? Upon the pillars.
The masters say: Upon twelve pillars.
And there are some who say: Upon seven pillars.
Rabbi Eleazar ben Shammua says:
Upon one pillar, and its name is "The Righteous."
For it is said: "But the righteous is the foundation of the
   world" (Prov.10:25).

CONCEPTION

Rabbi Hanina bar Pappa expounded:
The name of the angel appointed over conception is Night.
He takes the seed and lays it before the Holy One, blessed
   be he, and says to him:
Master of the universe, what is this seed to be —
mighty or weak, wise or foolish, rich or poor?
But he does not say "wicked or righteous."
So according to Rabbi Hanina. For Rabbi Hanina said:
All is in the hands of heaven, except the fear of heaven.

IT WERE BETTER

Our masters have taught:

For two years and a half there was a difference between the
school of Shammai and the school of Hillel.

The one school said:

It were better for a man not to have been created than to
have been created.

And the other school said:

It were better for a man to have been created than not to
have been created.

They voted and concluded:

It were better for a man not to have been created than to
have been created;

now that he has been created, let him search his deeds.

YOUR WORLD

In the hour when the Holy One, blessed be he, created the
first man,

he took him and let him pass before all the trees of the garden
of Eden,

and said to him:

See my works, how fine and excellent they are!

Now all that I have created for you have I created.

Think upon this, and do not corrupt and desolate my world;

for if you corrupt it, there is no one to set it right after you.

SINGULARITY

Therefore was man created single, to teach you
that whosoever wreck a single soul in Israel

the Writ considers to have wrecked a complete world,
and whosoever sustain a single soul in Israel
the Writ considers to have sustained a complete world;
and he was created single to keep peace among the human
creatures:
that no man might say to his fellow,
My father was greater than your father.

THE SOUL

"Bless the Lord, O my soul" (Ps.103:1).
As with the soul, no man knows the place where it is to be
found,
so with the Holy One, blessed be he — no man knows the
place where he is to be found.
David said:
Let the soul whose place no man knows
come and give praise to Him who is above his world,
and whose place no man knows.
The soul is one-and-only in the body, and the Holy One,
blessed be he, is one-and-only in his world.
Let the soul which is one-and-only in the body
come and give praise to the Holy One, blessed be he, who is
one-and-only in his world.

UNIQUE

See how many animals there are in the world, and how many
beasts there are in the world, and how many fish there
are in the world.
Is the voice of any one of them like the voice of any other?
Or the appearance of any one of them like the appearance of
any other?

Or the sense of any one of them like the sense of any other?
Or the taste of any one of them like the taste of any other?
Why, neither in voice, nor in appearance, nor in sense, nor
     in taste are they alike.
The masters have taught:
This is to tell you the greatness of the King who is king over
     all kings, the Holy One, blessed be he:
For a man stamps many coins in one mold and they are all
     alike;
but the King who is king over all kings, the Holy One, blessed
     be he, stamped every man in the mold of the first man,
yet not one of them resembles his fellow.
Hence, it is said:
"How great are Thy works, O Lord" (Ps.92:6).

IF NOT FOR THE WILL TO EVIL

"And God saw every thing that He had made, and behold, it
     was very good" (Gen.1:31).
Rav Nahman said in the name of Rav Samuel:
"Behold, it was very good" — that is the will to evil.
But is the will to evil good? That is astonishing!
Yet were it not for the will to evil,
men would not build homes, or take wives, or propagate,
     or engage in business.
And Solomon said the same:
"I considered all labour and all excelling in work,
that it is a man's rivalry with his neighbour" (Eccles.4:4).

. . . They said:
This being a time of good will, let us pray and ask for the
     will to evil.
They prayed and the will to evil was delivered to them.

The prophet said to them:
Know, if you destroy this one, the world will come to an end.
They imprisoned it for three days:
then they sought a new-laid egg in all the land of Israel,
and not one could be found.

THE IRON AND THE TREES

When iron was created, the trees began to tremble.
Said iron to them:
Why do you tremble? Let none of your wood enter me, and
not one of you will be injured.

HEAVEN AND EARTH

Our masters have taught:
The school of Shammai say:
Heaven was created first and afterward the earth was created;
for it is said: "In the beginning God created the heaven and
the earth" (Gen.1:1).
But the school of Hillel say:
The earth was created first and afterward heaven;
for it is said: "In the day the Lord God created earth and
heaven" (Gen.2:4).

The school of Hillel said to the school of Shammai:
According to what you say, first a man builds an upper story
and then he builds the house;
for it is said: "It is He that buildeth His upper chambers
in the heaven" (Amos 9:6).
The school of Shammai said to the school of Hillel:

According to what you say, first a man makes a footstool and
    then he makes the throne;
for it is said: "Thus saith the Lord: The heaven is My throne,
    and the earth is My footstool" (Isa.66:1).

But the masters say:
They were both created at once;
for it is said:
"Yea, My hand hath laid the foundation of the earth,
and My right hand hath spread out the heavens;
when I call unto them, they stand up together" (Isa.48:13).

THE ORDER OF THINGS

Ben Azzai said:
You will be called by your name,
you will be seated in your place,
you will be given what is yours.
No man touches what is meant for his fellow.
No kingdom touches its neighbor by so much as a
    hairsbreadth.

II

EVERY DAY

Every day man is sold, and every day redeemed.
Every day man's spirit is taken from him and given to the
    Keeper, and it is returned to him in the morning.
Every day miracles are worked for him as for those who went
    out of Egypt.
Every day redemption is worked for him, as for those who
    went out of Egypt.
Every day he is fed on the breasts of his mother.
Every day he is chastised for his deeds, like a child by his
    teacher.

LADDERS

A certain Roman matron asked Rabbi Yose ben Halafta:
In how many days did the Holy One, blessed be he, create
    his world?

He said to her: In six days.
She said to him: What has He been doing since that time?
He said to her:
The Holy One, blessed be he, is sitting and making ladders.
He raises this man and lowers that,
he humbles this man, and enriches that.

BEAUTY

Rav said:
A man is forbidden to say:
How beautiful is this alien woman!
Objection was taken:
Once Rabban Simeon ben Gamaliel was standing on a step
     of the mountain of the Temple,
and saw an alien woman who was exceptionally beautiful.
He said: "How manifold are thy works, O Lord!" (Ps.104:24).
— Rabban Simeon was merely giving thanks to God.
For a master said:
He who sees goodly creatures says:
Blessed is He in whose world are such creatures as these!

VESSELS

The daughter of the Roman Emperor said to Rabbi Joshua
     ben Hananiah:
O, wonderful wisdom in so ugly a vessel!
He said to her: Does your father keep wine in an earthen-
     ware jug?
She said to him: In what else should he keep it?
He said to her: You who are great folk ought to keep your
     wine in vessels of gold and silver!

She went and told her father. He had the wine put into vessels
   of gold and silver, and it turned sour.
They came and told the Emperor about it.
He said to his daughter: Who told you to do this?
She said to him: Rabbi Joshua ben Hananiah.
The Emperor called Rabbi Joshua and said to him: Why did
   you tell her to do so?
He said to him: I told her what she told me.
— And are there no handsome scholars?
— If they were ugly, they would be even more scholarly!

BEAUTY THAT WITHERS

Rabbi Eliezer was sick. Rabbi Yohanan came to visit him.
He saw Rabbi Eliezer lying in a dark house.
Rabbi Yohanan bared his arm, and the room lit up.
He saw that Rabbi Eliezer was crying. He said to him: Why
   are you crying?
Is it for the Torah in which you have not learned enough?
We have learned: Do more, do less, it matters not,
so long as one's heart is turned to heaven.
If because of the provisions you lack —
not every man merits two tables.
If because of the sons you have not —
see, this is the bone of my tenth son.
Rabbi Eliezer said to him:
I am crying over this beauty of yours, which is to wither in
   the dust.
He said to him:
You are right to cry over that.
And they wept together.

GROW!

Rabbi Simon said:
There is no grass without its own guardian star in the firmament
which strikes it and says to it, Grow!

PLANTING

At the beginning of the creation of the world, the Holy One,
blessed be he, began with planting first.
For it is written:
"And the Lord God planted a garden eastward in Eden"
(Gen.2:8).
You too when you enter the land shall engage in nothing but
planting.
Therefore it is written:
"And when ye shall come into the land, ye shall have
planted . . ." (Lev.19:23).

GREETING THE MESSIAH

Rabban Yohanan ben Zakkai used to say:
If there be a plant in your hand when they say to you:
Behold the Messiah!
— Go and plant the plant, and afterward go out to greet him.

A HELP MEET

Rabbi Yose happened upon Elijah.
He said to him:

It is written: "I will make him a help meet for him" (Gen.
2:18) —
how is a woman a help meet for a man?
He said to him: If a man bring wheat, does he chew wheat?
Flax — does he wear flax?
Does it not result that she enlightens his eyes, and sets him
on his feet?

THREE

In the past Adam was created from the earth and Eve was
created from Adam; from then, "in our image, after
our likeness" (Gen.1:26):
Neither man without woman
nor woman without man,
nor the two of them without the Divine Presence.

GO DOWN, GO UP

Go down a step, and take a wife.
Go up a step, and choose a friend.

DEMANDS

The woman demands with her heart
and the man demands with his mouth.
This is a good quality in women.

THE GENERATIONS OF MAN

Rabbi Judah bar Simon said:
While the first man still lay an unformed mass before Him
who spoke and the world came to be,

He showed him every generation and its interpreters,
every generation and its sages,
every generation and its scribes,
every generation and its leaders.

THE WILL

Everything is foreseen
and everything is laid bare
yet everything is in accordance with the will of man.

THE LIGHT THAT WAS HID

Rabbi Eleazar said:

The light which the Holy One, blessed be he, created on the
first day

— with it a man could look from one end of the world to the
other.

But when the Holy One, blessed be he, regarded the generation of the Flood and the generation of the division at
the Tower of Babel, and saw that their works were corrupt,

he arose and hid that light from them.

IN YOUR POWER

The Holy One, blessed be he, who is called righteous and
upright,

created man in his image only that he might be righteous
and upright like Him.

And should you say:

Why did he create the will to evil? It is written of man:

"For the imagination of man's heart is evil from his youth"
(Gen.8:21).

Since it says he is evil, who can make him good?

— The Holy One, blessed be he, says: It is you who make him
evil.

Why? A child of five, or six, or seven, or eight, or nine, does
not sin;

but from ten on, a will to evil springs up in him.

And if you should say: man cannot guard himself —

the Holy One, blessed be he, says:

There are many things in the world harder than the will to
evil, and more bitter, yet you make them sweet.

You have nothing more bitter than lupine,

yet you are diligent to boil it, and soak it seven times in water,
until it becomes sweet;

and the same with mustard and the caper plant, and many
other things.

So, if you can make the bitter things I have created sweet, for
your needs,

how much more can you do with the will to evil, which is in
your power.

THE SCALES

Our masters have taught:

Let a man ever view himself as though he were half guilty
and half worthy.

If he does one good deed, happy is he, for he has weighted
the balance in his favor.

If he commits one transgression, woe is him, for he has
weighted the balance against him.

Rabbi Eleazar bar Simeon says:

Because the world is judged after its majority,

and man is judged after the majority of his deeds:

If he does one good deed, happy is he, for he has weighted the balance in his favor and that of the whole world.

If he commits one transgression, woe is him, for he has weighted the balance against him and against the whole world.

SUBDUAL

"Thy righteousness is like the mighty mountains; Thy judgments are like the great deep" (Ps.36:7).

Rabbi Josiah the Great says:

Do not read it so, but transpose the Writ:

"Thy righteousness is on Thy judgments, as the mighty mountains on the great deep"

— as the mountains press down the deep that it may not rise and flood the world,

so righteous deeds press iniquities down

that all who come into the world may not be lost on the Day of Judgment.

MAN'S DEEDS

I call heaven and earth to witness:

whether it be heathen or Israelite,

whether it be man or woman, man-servant or maid-servant,

all according to his deeds

does the holy spirit rest upon a man.

Our masters have taught:

Once the daughter of Nehunia who dug wells for pilgrims
fell into a deep pit.

They went and told Rabbi Hanina ben Dosa.

The first hour he said to them: She is at ease.

The second hour he said: She is at ease.

The third hour he said: She has come out.

She was asked: Who fetched you up?

She said: A ram happened along, and an old man leading
him.

They asked Rabbi Hanina: Are you a prophet?

He said: I am neither a prophet, nor the son of a prophet,
but I said to myself: Shall that which this righteous man
troubles himself with, be a stumbling block to his seed?

Rabbi Aha said: Nevertheless, the well-digger's son died of
thirst.

LUCK

Raba said:

Long life, children, and sustenance depend not on merit,
but on luck.

Here Rabbah and Rav Hisda were both pious masters; one
master would pray and rain would fall, and the other
would pray and rain would fall;

Rav Hisda lived ninety and two years — Rabbah lived forty;
in the house of Rav Hisda were sixty wedding feasts — in
the house of Rabbah sixty bereavements;

in the house of Rav Hisda there was fine bread for the dogs,

and they would not eat it — in the house of Rabbah
there was barley for bread, and there was not enough for
the people.

RETRIBUTION

Hillel saw a skull floating on the water.
He said to it:
Because you drowned others, they have drowned you;
and the end of those that drowned you is that they shall be
drowned.

THE BITTER OLIVE

"And the dove came in to him at eventide; and lo in her
mouth an olive-leaf freshly plucked" (Gen.8:11).
Whence did she bring it?
Rabbi Bebai said: The gates of the garden of Eden opened;
she brought it from there.
Rabbi Aibo said to him:
If she brought it from the garden of Eden,
ought she not to have brought something superior, like cin-
namon or balsam?
But with the olive she gave a hint to Noah and said to him:
Master Noah, rather this bitter thing from the hand of the
Holy One, blessed be he,
than a sweet thing from your hand.

THE VINEYARD

When Noah came to plant a vineyard, Satan came and stood
before him.

He said to him: What are you planting?

He said to him: A vineyard.

He said to him: What is it like?

He said to him: Its fruit is sweet, wet or dry, and wine is made from it which delights the heart.

Satan said to him: Come, let us join together in the vineyard.

He said to him: Very well.

What did Satan do?

He brought a sheep and killed it under the vine.

After that he brought a lion and killed it,

and then he brought a pig and killed it.

And after that he brought a monkey and killed it under the vine,

and he sprinkled all the blood in that vineyard,

and watered it with the blood.

Thus Satan hinted to Noah

that before drinking of the wine a man is innocent, like a blameless sheep.

Once he had drunk enough, he is as brave as a lion, and says: There is none like me in all the world!

When he has drunk more than enough, he becomes a pig,

and befouls himself with excrement.

When he becomes drunk, he becomes a monkey,

and begins to dance, and says foul things,

and does not know what he is doing.

I AM THE MASTER

Rabbi Isaac said:

A man was wandering from place to place and saw a castle on fire.

He said: It seems this castle is without a master.

Then the master of the castle looked out at him and said:
  I am the master of the castle.
So, when Abraham said: It seems the world is without a
  master,
the Holy One, blessed be he, looked out at him and said to
  him,
I am the master of the world.

ABRAHAM'S CHOICE

"Unto thy seed will I give this land" (Gen.12:7).
Rabbi Levi said:
Journeying through Aram Naharaim and Aram Nahor,
Abraham saw the people eating and drinking and carousing.
He said: May I have no portion in this land!
But when he reached the Ladder of Tyre,
he saw the people busy
weeding in weeding time,
hoeing in hoeing time.
He said: May my portion fall in this land!
The Holy One, blessed be he, said to him:
"Unto thy seed will I give this land."

AS DUST

"And I will make thy seed as the dust of the earth" (Gen.
  13:16).
As the dust of the earth extends from one end of the world
  to the other,
so your children will be scattered from one end of the world
  to the other.

And as the dust of the earth can be blessed only through
    water,
So Israel too can be blessed only in virtue of the Torah,
    which is compared to water.
And as dust is made to be trampled on,
so your children too will be made for kingdoms to trample on.
And as dust wears vessels of metal away, but itself endures
    forever,
so with Israel: All the idolatrous nations shall be nought,
    but they shall endure.

SEED

"To be a God unto thee and to thy seed after thee" (Gen.
    17:7).
When there is "seed after thee," the Divine Presence rests
    upon thee.
When there is no "seed after thee," upon whom should it
    rest?
Upon the trees and upon the stones?

WORLD AND JUSTICE

"Shall not the Judge of all the earth do justly?" (Gen.18:25).
Rabbi Levi said:
If it is the world you seek, there can be no justice;
and if it is justice you seek, there can be no world.
Why do you grasp the rope by both ends,
seeking both the world and justice?
Let one of them go,
for if you do not relent a little, the world cannot endure.

NO DISTINCTION

Rabbi Samuel bar Nahmani said in the name of Rabbi Jonathan:

Catastrophe comes upon the world only when there are wicked persons in it —

and it begins with the righteous first.

Rabbi Joseph taught:

Once the Destroyer has been given permission to destroy, he does not distinguish between the righteous and the wicked;

what is more — he begins with the righteous first.

Rabbi Joseph wept:

Are the righteous as nothing?

Abayyi said to him: They are the first for their own good;

as it is said: "That the righteous is taken away from the evil to come" (Isa.57:1).

MOMENT OF JUDGMENT

"What aileth thee, Hagar? fear not; for God hath heard the voice of the lad where he is" (Gen.21:17).

Rabbi Isaac said:

Man is judged only by his deeds at the moment of judgment; for it is said of Ishmael:

"For God hath heard the voice of the lad where he is."

Rabbi Simon said:

The ministering angels leaped to denounce Ishmael.

They said to God:

Master of the universe, do you cause a well to spring for a man

whose children are destined to make your children die of
thirst?

He said to them:

What is he now, righteous or wicked?

They said to him: Righteous.

He said to them:

I judge a man only by his deeds at the moment of his judgment.

" 'Arise, lift up the lad. . . .' And God opened her eyes and
she saw a well of water; and she went, and filled the
bottle with water, and gave the lad drink" (Gen.21:18–
19).

THE VOICE AND THE HANDS

"The voice is the voice of Jacob, but the hands are the hands
of Esau" (Gen.27:22).

The nations of the world entered before Abnimos the weaver.
They said to him:

Can we attack this nation?

He said to them:

Go and pass before their Houses of Study and Houses of
Prayer.

If you there hear children chanting, you cannot attack them.

But if you do not hear children chanting, you can attack
them.

For thus their father assured them:

"The voice is the voice of Jacob":

So long as the voice of Jacob is chanting in Houses of Study
and Houses of Prayer,

the hands are not "the hands of Esau."

"And he dreamed, and behold a ladder set up on the earth,
and the top of it reaching to heaven; and behold the
angels of God ascending and descending on it" (Gen.
28:12).

— Teaching us that the Holy One, blessed be he, showed to
our father Jacob

the lord of Babylonia ascending and descending,

and the lord of Medea ascending and descending,

and the lord of Greece ascending and descending,

and the lord of Rome ascending and descending.

The Holy One, blessed be he, said to him: Jacob, you must
ascend too!

Then our father Jacob grew very fearful and said:

But perhaps, as they shall have to descend, I, too, shall have
to descend.

The Holy One, blessed be he, said to him:

"Be not dismayed, O Israel" (Jer.30:10). If you ascend, you
shall never have to descend.

But Jacob did not have faith, and did not ascend.

The Holy One, blessed be he, said to him:

If you had had faith and ascended, you would never have
descended again.

But now that you have not had faith, and have not ascended,

your children will be enslaved to four kingdoms in this world,

through duties, taxes in kind, fines, and poll taxes.

Then Jacob grew very fearful and said to the Holy One,
blessed be he: Will that last forever?

He said to him (ibid.): "Be not dismayed, O Israel,

for behold I will save thee from afar" — from Babylonia.

"And thy seed from the land of their captivity will return"
— from Gaul and Spain and the neighboring lands.
"And Israel shall return" — from Babylonia.
"And be quiet" — from Medea.
"And at ease" — from Greece.
"And none shall make him afraid" — from Rome.

THE IMAGE IN THE WINDOW

"And Joseph was brought down to Egypt; and Potiphar, an
officer of Pharaoh's . . . bought him of the hand of the
Ishmaelites. . . . And it came to pass . . . that his master's wife cast her eyes upon Joseph. . . . And it came to
pass on a certain day . . . that she caught him by his garment, saying: Lie with me" (Gen.39:1, 7, 11, 12).
At that moment the image of his father appeared to him in
the window.
He said to him:
Joseph, your brothers' names are destined to be written on
the stones of the ephod,
and your name among them.
Do you wish your name erased from its place among theirs,
and yourself to be called the companion of whores?

IV

THORNBUSH

A certain heathen asked Rabbi Joshua ben Karhah:
Why did the Holy One, blessed be he, speak to Moses out of a
thornbush?
He said to him: Had it been out of a carob, or out of a syca-
more, you would ask the same question.
But I cannot send you away empty-handed.
Well then: Why out of a thornbush?
To teach you that there is no space free of the Divine Pres-
ence, not even a thornbush.

Rabbi Yohanan said:
Just as thornbushes are made into garden fences,
so Israel is the fence of the world.

SIGNS

This people is known by three signs:
Being compassionate, shamefaced, and charitable.
Everyone who has these three signs is worthy of cleaving to
this people.

"Thy name is as oil poured forth" (Cant.1:3).

As oil is bitter to begin with, but sweet in the end,

so: "And though thy beginning was small, yet thy end should
greatly increase" (Job 8:7).

As oil improves only through being pressed,

so Israel cannot turn from sin,

except through chastisement.

As oil which when a drop of water falls into a full cup of oil,
a drop of the oil spills out,

so, when a word of Torah enters the heart, a word of scoffing
leaves it;

when a word of scoffing enters the heart, a word of Torah
leaves it.

As oil brings light to the world,

so Israel is the light of the world;

as it is said: "And nations shall walk at thy light, and kings at
the brightness of thy rising" (Isa.60:3).

As oil is soundless,

so Israel is soundless in this world.

CROSSING THE RIVER

Rabbi Pinhas ben Yair was going to the House of Study, but
the river Ginnai was too strong for him.

He said to it:

Ginnai, Ginnai, why do you keep me from the House of
Study?

It parted before him, and he passed.

His disciples said to him: Could we pass too?

37

He said to them:
He who knows in his heart that he has never injured any man
in Israel can pass without harm.

COMMUNITY

Our masters have taught:
When Israel is sunk in sorrow, if one of Israel should separate
from them, the two ministering angels that accompany
every man come and place their hands on his head and
say:
So and so has separated from the community; let him not see
the consolation of the community.

SHARING

Rabbi Yohanan said:
Every distress that Israel and the nations of the world share
is a distress indeed.
Every distress that is Israel's alone
is no distress.

THE YOKE OF FREEDOM

Had Israel gazed deep into the words of the Torah when it
was given them,
no nation or kingdom could ever rule over them.
And what did it say to them?
Accept upon yourselves the yoke of the kingdom of heaven,
and subdue one another in the fear of heaven,
and deal with one another in charity.

"And he said: If thou wilt diligently hearken . . ." (Exod.
    15:26).

Rabbi Eleazar of Modim says:

"If thou wilt diligently hearken"

— this is the principle in which the whole Torah is contained.

"To the voice of the Lord thy God"

— teaching us that whoever hearkens to the mouth of his
    Master,

the Writ considers to be standing and serving

before Him who lives and endures forever and evermore.

"And wilt do that which is right in His eyes"

— that is, in commerce,

teaching us that whoever deals in good faith,

his fellow creatures take pleasure in him,

and he is considered to be fulfilling the whole Torah.

SUSTENANCE

"And the people shall go out and gather a day's portion every
    day" (Exod.16:4).

He that created the day created the sustenance of the day.

Hence, Rabbi Eleazar of Modim used to say:

He that has something to eat today, and says, What shall I eat
    tomorrow — lo, he is lacking in faith.

For it is said: "That I may prove them, whether they will walk
    in My law, or not" (*ibid.*).

BEFORE YOU

"And the Lord said unto Moses . . . Behold I will stand before thee there upon the rock in Horeb" (Exod.17:5–6).
The Holy One, blessed be he, said to him:
Wherever you find the mark of a man's foot,
there I am before you.

FOR ALL TO SEE

The Torah was given in public, for all to see, in the open.
For if it had been given in the land of Israel, Israel would
have said to the nations of the world, You have no share
in it;
therefore the Torah was given in the wilderness, in public,
for all to see, in the open,
and everyone who wishes to receive it, let him come and receive it.

THE WAY OF FIRE

"Now mount Sinai was altogether on smoke, because the
Lord descended upon it in fire" (Exod.19:18)
— Telling us that the Torah is fire, and was given in the midst
of fire, and is compared to fire.
As the way of fire is, that when a man is near it, he is burned,
when far from it, chilled —
so the only way for a man to do is to warm himself in the light.

ALL AT ONE TIME

"And God spoke all these words" (Exod.20:1).
— All at one and the same time:
killing and giving life at one and the same time,

afflicting and healing at one and the same time.

Answering the woman in her travail,

those who go down to the sea and the desert farers,

those locked in the prison house,

one in the east and one in the west, one in the north, and one in the south;

"Forming the light, and creating darkness; making peace and creating evil" (Isa.45:7),

— all at one and the same time.

Dust is turned into man, and man is turned into dust;

as it is said:

"And turneth the shadow of death into morning" (Amos 5:8).

THE VOICE

Rabbi Abbahu said in the name of Rabbi Yohanan:

When the Holy One, blessed be he, gave the Torah,

not a bird cried, not a fowl flew, not an ox bellowed, the angels did not fly, the seraphim did not say, Holy, Holy, the sea did not stir, the human creatures did not speak,

but the world was still and silent,

and the voice went forth:

"I am the Lord thy God" (Exod.20:2).

TO ME THE WORD

"I am the Lord thy God" (Exod.20:2).

Rabbi Levi said:

The Holy One, blessed be he, appeared to them as a statue which can be seen everywhere.

A thousand men gaze at it, and it gazes back at all.

So looked the Holy One, blessed be he, when he was speaking to Israel.

Each and every one of Israel said to himself:
It is to me the Word is speaking.

TWO VIEWS

Raba said:
All that Ezekiel saw, Isaiah saw.
What was Ezekiel like? Like a countryman who saw the king.
And what was Isaiah like? Like a townsman who saw the king.

GUARANTORS

When Israel stood to receive the Torah,
the Holy One, blessed be he, said to them:
I am giving you my Torah. Bring me good guarantors that
    you will guard it, and I shall give it to you.
They said: Our fathers are our guarantors.
The Holy One, blessed be he, said to them:
Your fathers are unacceptable to me.
Abraham is unacceptable who said: "Whereby shall I know"
    (Gen.15:8).
Isaac is unacceptable to me, because he loved Esau and I
    hated him,
and Jacob is unacceptable who said: "My way is hid from the
    Lord" (Isa.40:27).
Yet bring me good guarantors, and I shall give it to you.
They said to him:
Master of the universe, our prophets are our guarantors.
He said to them:
The prophets are unacceptable to me:
"The rulers transgressed against Me; the prophets also proph-
    esied by Baal" (Jer.2:8).

Yet bring me good guarantors, and I shall give it to you.
They said:
Behold, our children are our guarantors.
The Holy One, blessed be he, said:
They are certainly good guarantors.
For their sake I give the Torah to you.

TEAR DOWN

Rabbi Simeon ben Eleazar says:
If old men tell you, Tear down, and young men tell you,
    Build up,
tear down, and do not build up.
For the destruction of the old men is construction,
and the construction of the young men destruction.

NOT MEANT FOR ANGELS

Rabbi Joshua ben Levi said:
When Moses ascended to heaven, the ministering angels said
    to the Holy One, blessed be he: What is a man born of
    woman doing here?
He said to them: He has come to receive the Torah.
They said to Him: Is it the precious hidden treasure which
    first you hid nine hundred and seventy-four generations
    before the world was created that you seek to give to
    flesh and blood?
"What is man, that Thou art mindful of him? And the son of
    man, that Thou thinkest of him?
O Lord, our Lord, How glorious is Thy name in all the earth!
Whose majesty is rehearsed above the *heavens*" (Ps.8:5, 2).
The Holy One, blessed be he, said to Moses:

Reply to them. . . .

Moses said to Him:

Master of the universe, what is written in this Torah which
you are about to give me?

"I am the Lord thy God who brought thee out of the land of
Egypt" (Exod.20:2):

Moses said to the angels:

Did *you* go down to Egypt? Were *you* enslaved to Pharaoh?
Then what is the Torah to you?

What else is written in it?

"Thou shalt have no other gods" (*ibid.* v.3):

Are *you* surrounded by nations that worship other gods?

What else is written in it?

"Remember the sabbath day, to keep it holy" (*ibid.* v.8):

Do *you* do any labor, that you need to rest?

What else is written in it?

"Thou shalt not take the name of the Lord thy God in vain"
(*ibid.* v.7):

Is there any commerce, any give and take among *you?*

What else is written in it?

"Honour thy father and thy mother" (*ibid.* v.12):

Do *you* have fathers and mothers?

What else is written in it?

"Thou shalt not murder. Thou shalt not commit adultery.
Thou shalt not steal" (*ibid.* v.13):

Is there any jealousy in *your* midst? Is there any will to evil
in *your* midst?

At once they conceded to the Holy One, blessed be he.

As it is written:

"O Lord, our Lord, How glorious is Thy name in all the
earth!" (Ps.8:2).

44

Rabbi Yohanan wept when he came to this verse:

"Behold, He putteth no trust in His saints" (Job 15:15).

If He putteth no trust in His saints, in whom does he put trust?

One day he was going on a journey and saw a man gathering figs. He was leaving those that were ripe, and taking those that were green.

Rabbi Yohanan said to the man: Are not those better?

The man said to him:

I need them to take on a journey; these can keep, those cannot keep.

Rabbi Yohanan said:

This is why it is written: "Behold, He putteth no trust in His saints."

THE NATIONS REFUSE THE TORAH

When the Omnipresent revealed himself to give the Torah to Israel,

he revealed himself not to Israel alone, but to all the nations.

At first he went to the children of Esau, and said to them:

Will you accept the Torah?

They said to him: What is written in it?

He said to them: "Thou shalt not kill."

They said to him: Master of the universe, our father was a killer by nature;

as it is said: ". . . but the hands are the hands of Esau" (Gen. 27:22);

in this he was confirmed by his father;

as it is said: "And by thy sword shalt thou live" (Gen.27:40).

45

Then He went to the children of Ammon and Moab and said
   to them:
Will you accept the Torah?
They said to him: What is written in it?
He said to them: "Thou shalt not commit adultery."
They said to him: Master of the universe, immorality is our
   nature. . . .

He went and found the children of Ishmael, and said to them:
Will you accept the Torah?
They said to him: What is written in it?
He said to them: "Thou shalt not steal."
They said to him: Master of the universe, our father was a
   thief by nature;
as it is said: "And he shall be a wild ass of a man" (Gen.
   16:12).

There was not a nation of all the nations to whom He did not
   go, and to whom he did not speak, and on whose threshold he did not knock, to ask whether they wished to receive the Torah. . . .
But even the seven commandments which the children of
   Noah did accept they could not persevere in,
until he lifted their yoke off them, and gave them to Israel.

INDIFFERENT LOVE

"Therefore do the maidens love thee" (Cant.1:3).
Even the nations of the world who recognize wisdom and
   understanding and knowledge and intelligence,
and attain to the substance of your Torah,
"love thee" with a perfect love —
whether He is good to them, whether He is bad to them.

46

There is no creature the Holy One, blessed be he, rejects,
but he accepts them all.
The gates are open at every hour,
and all who wish to enter, may enter.
Therefore it is said:
"My doors I opened to the wanderer" (Job 31:32)
— meaning the Holy One, blessed be he, who suffers his crea-
    tures.

V

WITNESSES

"And ye are My witnesses, saith the Lord, and I am God"
(Isa.43:12).
Rabbi Simeon ben Yohai taught:
If ye are "my witnesses," I am the Lord,
and if ye are not my witnesses,
I am not, as it were, the Lord.

WHERE IS THE TORAH

Rabbi Joshua ben Levi said:
When Moses descended from the presence of the Holy One,
blessed be he, Satan came and said to Him:
Master of the universe, where is the Torah?

He said to him: I have given it to the earth.

Satan went to earth and said to her: Where is the Torah?

She said to him: "God understandeth the way thereof" (Job 28:23).

He went to the sea, and she said to him: "It is not with me."

He went to the deep. It said to him: "It is not in me."

As it is written: "The deep saith: 'It is not in me'; and the sea saith: 'It is not with me.' Destruction and Death say: 'We have heard a rumour thereof with our ears' " (Job 28:14,22).

Satan returned and said to the Holy One, blessed be he:

Master of the universe, I have sought the Torah over all the earth, and have not found it.

He said to him: Go to the son of Amram.

Satan went to Moses and said to him:

Where is the Torah which the Holy One, blessed be he, gave to you?

He said to him:

What am I, that the Holy One, blessed be he, should give me the Torah?

The Holy One, blessed be he, said to Moses:

Moses, are you a liar?

Moses said to him:

Master of the universe, you have a precious hidden treasure which you delight in every day —

dare I say it is mine?

The Holy One, blessed be he, said to Moses:

Because you have belittled yourself, it shall be called after you;

as it is said: "Remember ye the *law of Moses* My servant" (Mal.3:22).

PREPARATION

Let a man do good deeds, and then ask Torah from the Omnipresent.
Let a man do righteous and fitting deeds, and then ask wisdom from the Omnipresent.
Let a man seize the way of humility, and then ask understanding from the Omnipresent.

IMITATION

Rav Joseph said:
Ever let a man learn from the wise ways of his Creator.
For lo, the Holy One, blessed be he, left all the mountains
   and hills, and settled his Presence on Mount Sinai,
and left all the goodly trees, and settled his Presence on the
   thornbush.

HUMILITY

Thus said the Holy One, blessed be he, to Israel:
My children, have I allowed you to lack?
What do I seek of you?
All I ask is that you love one another,
and honor one another, and respect one another,
and let there be found in you neither transgression nor theft
   nor any ugly thing;
so that you never become tainted;
as it is said: "It hath been told thee, O man, what is good
   . . . and to walk humbly with thy God" (Mic.6:8)
— do not read: "Walk humbly with thy God,"
but rather: "Walk humbly, and thy God will be with thee"

—as long as you are with him in humility,
he will be with you in humility.

THREE THINGS

Raba said:
Three things I asked of heaven;
two were given me, one was not given me.
The wisdom of Rav Huna and the wealth of Rav Hisda were
given me;
the humility of Rabba bar Rav Huna was not given me.

THY WORDS BE FEW

Rav Huna quoted Rav as saying in the name of Rabbi Meir,
and we have learned the same in the name of Rabbi Akiba:
Let a man ever say:
All that the Compassionate One does, he does for the best.
Rav Huna quoted Rav as saying in the name of Rabbi Meir:
Let a man's words ever be few before the Holy One, blessed
be he.
For it is said:
"Be not rash with thy mouth, and let not thy heart be hasty
to utter a word before God; for God is in heaven, and
thou upon earth; therefore let thy words be few" (Eccles.
5:1).

NOT TOGETHER

Rav Hisda said, and some say Mar Ukba:
Of every man whose spirit is haughty, the Holy One, blessed
be he, says:
He and I cannot dwell together in the world.

MAN'S HOUR

Everyone that humbles himself the Holy One, blessed be he,
 lifts up;
and everyone that lifts himself up the Holy One, blessed be
 he, humbles.
Everyone that pursues greatness, greatness flees;
and everyone that flees greatness, greatness pursues.
Everyone that pushes his hour ahead, his hour pushes him
 back;
And everyone that stands back for his hour, his hour stands
 by him.

AS THE DESERT

Why was the Torah given in the desert?
To teach you
that if a man does not hold himself as unpossessed as the
 desert,
he does not become worthy of the words of the Torah;
and that, as the desert has no end,
so with the words of the Torah:
there is no end to them.

AS WINE

As wine, which though it have the taste of wine when new,
 the longer it ages in the cask, the better it tastes —
so with the words of Torah:
the longer they age in the body, the older they are, the better;
as it is said:
"Wisdom is with aged men, and understanding in length of
 days" (Job 12:12).

And as wine cannot keep either in a gold vessel or in a silver,
but in that which is the poorest of all vessels, an earthen
vessel —
so the words of the Torah can keep only in one who makes
himself lowly.

LEARNING

Rav Nahman bar Isaac said:
Why are the words of the Torah compared to a tree,
as it is said: "She is a tree of life to them that lay hold upon
her" (Prov.3:18)?
This is to tell you
that as a small log may set fire to a large log,
so do the lesser scholars sharpen the wits of the greater.
And Rabbi Hanina said the same:
Much have I learned from my masters,
and more from my comrades than from my masters,
and from my disciples the most.

MAN'S LIMITS

Rabbi Isaac said:
If a man says to you, I have toiled and I have not found
— do not believe him.
I have not toiled and I have found
— do not believe him.
I have toiled and I have found
— believe him.
This holds only for the words of the Torah;
but in commerce man must rely on the aid of heaven.
And in the words of the Torah this holds only for sharpening
one's learning;

but in retaining what he has learned,
man must rely on the aid of heaven.

HE AND I

The masters of Yavneh were in a habit of saying:
I am a creature and my fellow man is a creature.
My work is in the city and his work is in the field.
I rise early to go to my work, and he rises early to go to his
    work.
As he does not pride himself on his work,
so I do not pride myself on mine.
But should you think that I am doing more than he —
we have learned:
"Do more, do less, it matters not,
so long as one's heart is turned to heaven."

THE WATCHMEN

Rabbi Judah the Prince sent Rabbi Dosa and Rabbi Ammi
    to travel to all the cities in the land of Israel and to in-
    spect them.
They came to one city and said to the people:
Let the watchmen of the city come here.
They brought out the chief of the city guard and the sheriff.
The rabbis said to them:
Are these the watchmen of the city? They are the destroyers
    of the city!
They said to them:
And who are the watchmen of the city?
They said to them:
They are the teachers of the Written Law and the teachers of
    the Oral Law,

54

for they watch day and night;

in keeping with the words:

"Thou shalt meditate therein day and night" (Josh.1:8).

SAVING THE TORAH

When Rabbi Hanina and Rabbi Hiyya fell into a dispute,

Rabbi Hanina said to Rabbi Hiyya:

Is it with me you are disputing? God forbid, if the Torah
should be forgotten in Israel, I would bring it back with
my reasoning!

Rabbi Hiyya said to Rabbi Hanina:

Is it with me you are disputing, I, who saved the Torah from
being forgotten in Israel?

What did I do? I went and sowed flax and made nets from it;
I caught deer, and gave their flesh to orphans; and I
made scrolls from the skins, and I copied the five books
of Moses on them. Then I went to a town and taught
the five books to five children, and instructed six children in the six orders of the Mishnah. And I said to
them: Until I come back, study the five books together
and instruct each other in the Mishnah. And thus I
saved the Torah from being forgotten in Israel.

This is why Rabbi Judah the Scribe said:

How great are the deeds of Hiyya!

THE ORAL LAW

Once I was on a journey, and I came upon a man who went
at me after the way of heretics.

Now, he accepted the Written, but not the Oral Law.

He said to me:

The Written Law was given us from Mount Sinai;

the Oral Law was not given us from Mount Sinai.

I said to him:

But were not both the Written and the Oral Law spoken by the Omnipresent?

Then what difference is there between the Written and the Oral Law? To what can this be compared?

To a king of flesh and blood who had two servants, and loved them both with a perfect love;

and he gave them each a measure of wheat, and each a bundle of flax.

The wise servant, what did he do?

He took the flax and spun a cloth.

Then he took the wheat and made flour.

The flour he cleansed, and ground, and kneaded, and baked, and set on top of the table.

Then he spread the cloth over it, and left it so until the king should come.

But the foolish servant did nothing at all.

After some days, the king returned from a journey and came into his house and said to them:

My sons, bring me what I gave you.

One servant showed the wheaten bread on the table with a cloth spread over it,

and the other servant showed the wheat still in the box, with a bundle of flax upon it.

Alas for his shame, alas for his disgrace!

Now, when the Holy One, blessed be he, gave the Torah to Israel,

he gave it only in the form of wheat, for us to extract flour from it,

and flax, to extract a garment.

It happened to Rabbah bar Bar Hanan that some porters
    broke a barrel of his wine.
He took away their cloaks.
They went and told Rav.
He said to him: Give them back their cloaks.
He said to him: Is that the law?
He said to him: Yes: "That thou mayest walk in the way of
    good men" (Prov.2:20).
He gave them back their cloaks.
They said to Rav: We are poor men, and have worked all
    day, and are in need, and have nothing.
He said to him: Go and pay them.
He said to him: Is that the law?
He said to him: Yes: "And keep the paths of the righteous"
    (*ibid.*).

STAND UP

Raba said:
How stupid people are, who stand up before a Torah Scroll
and do not stand up before a great man!

THE WAYS OF LIFE

When Rabbi Eliezer fell sick, his disciples came to visit him.
They said to him: Master, teach us the ways of life, that by
    following them we may be worthy of the world to come.
He said to them:
Be careful to respect your comrades,
and keep your children from superficiality

but sit them at the knees of scholars,

and when you are praying remember before Whom you are standing.

Then you shall be worthy of the world to come.

AS A DOG OR CROW

Rabbi Judah the Prince opened his granary in the years of drought. He said:

Let those who have studied the Torah enter, and those who have studied the Mishnah, those who have studied the Gemara, those who have studied the Halakhah, and those who have studied the Haggadah — but let no ig-noramus enter!

Rabbi Jonathan ben Amram pressed forward and entered. He said: Master, feed me!

Rabbi Judah said to him: Have you studied the Torah, my son?

He said: No.

Have you studied the Mishnah?

He said: No.

If so, how can I feed you?

He said: Feed me as you would a dog or a crow.

Rabbi Judah fed him. After he had gone, Rabbi Judah sat regretting what he had done and said: Alas, for I have given of my bread to an ignoramus.

Then Rabbi Simeon his son said to Rabbi Judah:

Perhaps that was Jonathan ben Amram, your disciple who has refused all his life to profit from the Torah.

They investigated, and found this to be so.

Rabbi Judah said: Let everyone enter.

Bar Kappara expounded:

Which is the small section in which all the principles of the
Torah are contained?

— "In all thy ways know Him

And He will direct thy paths" (Prov.3:6).

DAVID'S HARP

"At midnight I will rise to give thanks unto Thee" (Ps.119:
62).

Rabbi Pinhas said in the name of Rabbi Eleazar bar Mena-
hem:

What was it David used to do?

He would take a psaltery and harp, and place them at the
head of his bed, and rise up in the middle of the night
and play on them.

Then the sages of Israel would hear his voice and say:

If David, King of Israel, is engaging in the Torah,

how much more ought we!

It followed that all Israel engaged in the Torah through him.

Rabbi Levi said:

There was a window near David's bed, which opened on the
north,

and there was a harp hanging opposite it;

and the north wind would come out in the middle of the
night and blow on the harp,

and the harp would play of itself.

And all Israel would hear the sound and say:

If David, King of Israel, is engaging in Torah,
how much more ought we!
It followed that all Israel engaged in the Torah.

PATHS

This Torah is like two paths, one of sunlight, and one of
   snow.
Take the one and die of sun, take the other and die in the
   snow.
What to do? Walk between the two.

FATHERS AND CHILDREN

When the Holy One, blessed be he, said to Moses:
". . . visiting the iniquity of the fathers upon the children"
(Exod.20:5),
Moses said:
Many are the wicked who have begotten righteous children;
shall they take the consequences of their fathers' iniquities?
Terah served images, and Abraham his son was righteous,
the same with Hezekiah who was righteous, and Ahaz his
father wicked,
the same with Josiah who was righteous, and Amon his father
wicked.
Is it right then that the righteous be struck down for the iniquity of their fathers?
The Holy One, blessed be he, said:
By your life, I am voiding my words and fulfilling yours.
As it is said: "The fathers shall not be put to death for the
children, neither shall the children be put to death for
the fathers" (Deut.24:16).

And, by your life, I am writing them down in your name,
as it is said: "According to that which is written in the book
of the law of Moses" (II Kings 14:6).

FOUR ANSWERS

Wisdom was asked: The sinner, what is his destiny?
She said to those who asked: "Evil pursueth sinners" (Prov.
13:21).
Prophecy was asked: The sinner, what is his destiny?
She said to those who asked: "The soul that sinneth, it shall
die" (Ezek.18:4).
The Torah was asked: The sinner, what is his destiny?
She said to those who asked: Let him bring a guilt-offering,
and atonement shall be made for him;
as it is written: "And it shall be accepted for him to make
atonement for him" (Lev.1:4).
The Holy One, blessed be he, was asked:
The sinner, what is his destiny?
He said to those who asked:
Let him turn in repentance, and atonement shall be made for
him;
as it is written:
"Good and upright is the Lord; therefore doth He instruct
sinners in the way" (Ps.25:8).

THE BROKEN VESSEL

A man of flesh and blood, if he has a vessel,
so long as the vessel is whole, he is happy with it;
broken, he does not wish it.

But not so the Holy One, blessed be he.

So long as the vessel is whole, he does not wish to see it;

broken, he wishes it.

And what is the favorite vessel of the Holy One, blessed be
he?

The heart of man.

If the Holy One, blessed be he, sees a proud heart,

he does not wish it;

as it is said: "Every one that is proud in heart is an abomina-
tion to the Lord" (Prov.16:5).

— Broken, he says: This is mine;

as it is said: "The Lord is nigh unto them that are of a
broken heart" (Ps.34:19).

LABOR

Rabbi Eliezer used to say:

Labor is great;

for, as Israel were commanded to keep the Sabbath,

so they were commanded to labor;

as it is said: "Six days shalt thou labour, and do all thy work"
(Exod.20:9).

ADVICE

Rav said to Rav Kahana:

Traffic in carcasses, and do no traffic with words.

Flay carcasses in the market place for wages, and do not say:

I am a priest and a great man, and it is beneath me.

Climb the roof — but take your provisions with you.

SUSTENANCE

Rabbi Meir says:

Ever let a man teach his son a clean trade and an easy,

and then let him pray to Him to whom wealth and property
belong.

For there is no trade which does not bring either poverty or
wealth;

for the poverty does not come from the trade, and the wealth
does not come from the trade, but all is according to a
man's merit.

Rabbi Simeon ben Eleazar says:

Have you ever seen beast or fowl that have a trade, yet they
sustain themselves without trouble, though they were
created only to serve me —

and I was created to serve my Maker; how much more ought
I to sustain myself without trouble —

but I have acted wickedly, and have spoiled my sustenance.

PROVISION

I call heaven and earth to be my witness,

that the Holy One, blessed be he, is sitting and dividing provisions with his own hand

among all who come into the world,

and among all the handiwork that he created in the world;

from man to beast, to creeping thing, and to the bird in the
sky.

EQUAL IN HONOR

When a man curses his father and mother and beats them and
    deals them wounds,
the Holy One, blessed be he, folds his feet, as it were, under
    his throne of glory, and says:
I have likened my own glory to them,
for all three are equal with regard to honor.
If I were with this man, he would do the same to me.
I did well not to live with him.

RANSOM

If a man is in captivity with his father and his master,
he comes before his master,
his master comes before his father.
His mother comes before them all.

BLOOD

Someone came before Raba and said:
The mayor of my town has told me:
Go and kill so and so; if you do not, I will have you killed.
Raba said to him: Let him kill you, but you must not kill.
What do you think, your blood is redder than another man's?
Perhaps his blood is redder than yours.

ALTAR AND IRON

"And if thou make Me an altar of stone, thou shalt not build
    it of hewn stones, for if thou lift up thy tool upon it, thou
    hast profaned it" (Exod.20:22).

From this, Rabbi Simeon ben Eleazar used to say:

The altar was built to lengthen man's years,

and the iron to cut his years short.

It was not permitted to lift up that which cuts short upon
that which lengthens.

JESTERS

Rav Beroka of Be Hozae was often in the market at Be Lapat.

There he would meet Elijah. Once he said to Elijah:

Is there anyone in this market who shall have the world to
come?

Elijah said to him: No.

They were standing there when two men came along.

Elijah said to him: These shall have the world to come.

Rav Beroka went to them and said: What do you do?

They said to him:

We are jesters, and make the sad to laugh.

When we see two men quarreling,

we strain ourselves to make peace between them.

THE GUARDIAN OF CHASTITY

The masters saw in a dream how a donkey-driver prayed and
rain fell.

The masters sent for him, and he was brought before them.

They said to him: What is your trade?

He said to them: I am a donkey-driver.

They said to him: What good thing hàve you done?

He said to them:

Once I hired my donkey to a woman who was crying in the
street.

66

I said to her: What is the matter?
She said to me:
My husband is in prison, and I must do whatever I must in
  order to buy his freedom.
So I went and sold my donkey, and brought her the money;
  and I said to her:
Here it is; free your husband, and do not sin!
The masters said to him:
You are worthy to pray, and to be answered.

THEY THAT LOVE HIM

Our masters have taught:
They that are shamed, and do not shame others,
that hear their disgrace, and do not retort,
that act out of love, and rejoice in chastisements —
it is of them that the Writ says:
"But they that love Him be as the sun when he goeth forth
  in his might" (Judg.5:31).

VII

PRINCIPLES AND DETAILS

Rabbi Judah says:

Ever let a man grasp the words of the Torah in the round,

for if he grasps them in detail, they weary him, and he does
not know what to do with them.

Like a man going to Caesarea who needs one hundred zuz or
two hundred for expenses.

If he takes it in small coins, they weary him, and he does not
know what to do with them.

But if he puts them together and turns them into selas, he
can exchange and spend them wherever he desires.

THE ONE COMMANDMENT

Rabbi Simlai expounded:

Six hundred and thirteen commandments were given to
Moses,

three hundred and sixty-five "Thou shalt nots," the number
of the days of the solar year,

and two hundred and forty-eight "Thou shalts,"
corresponding to the parts of the body.

David came and brought them down to eleven;
as it is written:
"Lord, who shall sojourn in Thy tabernacle? . . .
He that walketh uprightly, and worketh righteousness, and
  speaketh truth in his heart; that hath no slander upon
  his tongue, nor doeth evil to his fellow, nor taketh up a
  reproach against his neighbour; in whose eyes a vile person is despised, but he honoureth them that fear the
  Lord; he that sweareth to his own hurt, and changeth
  not; he that putteth not out his money on interest, nor
  taketh a bribe against the innocent" (Ps.15:1-5).

Isaiah came and brought them down to six;
as it is written:
"He that walketh righteously and speaketh uprightly; he that
  despiseth the gain of oppressions, that shaketh his hands
  from holding of bribes, that stoppeth his ears from hear-
  ing of blood, and shutteth his eyes from looking upon
  evil" (Isa.33:15).

Micah came and brought them down to three;
as it is written:
"It hath been told thee, O man, what is good . . .: Only to
  do justly, and to love mercy, and to walk humbly with
  thy God" (Mic.6:8).

Isaiah came again and brought them down to two;
as it is said:
"Thus saith the Lord,

Keep ye justice, and do righteousness" (Isa.56:1).

Amos came and brought them down to one;
as it is said:
"For thus saith the Lord unto the house of Israel:
Seek ye Me, and live" (Amos 5:4).

Rav Nahman bar Isaac objected:
"Seek ye Me" — may it not mean: in all the Torah?
Rather Habakkuk came and brought them down to one;
as it is said:
"But the righteous shall live by his faith" (Hab.2:4).

THE CHOICE

Rabbi Simon said in the name of Rabbi Simeon ben Halafta:
Like a councilor who grew up in the house of a king.
The king said to him: Ask what I shall give thee.
The councilor said:
If I ask silver and gold, he will give them to me;
precious stones and jewels, he will give them to me.
He said:
Lo, I shall ask the daughter of the king, and all else will be
    included.
So:
"In Gibeon the Lord appeared to Solomon in a dream by
    night; and God said: 'Ask what I shall give thee'" (I
    Kings 3:5).
Solomon said:
If I ask silver and gold and precious stones and jewels, he
    will give them to me.
But lo, I shall ask wisdom, and all else will be included.

Therefore it is written:

"Give Thy servant therefore an understanding heart" (I
Kings 3:9).

The Holy One, blessed be he, said to him:

Solomon, you have asked wisdom for yourself and have not
asked wealth and goods and the life of your foes;

by your life, you are now given wisdom and knowledge,

and through them I shall give you wealth and goods as well.

THE EAR

"But if the servant shall plainly say: I love my master . . . I
will not go out free; then his master shall bring him unto
God, and shall bring him to the door, or unto the door-
post; and his master shall bore his ear through with an
awl; and he shall serve him for ever" (Exod.21:5–6).

Rabban Yohanan ben Zakkai would expound a principle
from this verse.

Why is the ear chosen of all the parts of the body?

The Holy One, blessed be he, said:

This ear heard my voice on Mount Sinai when I said:

"For unto Me the children of Israel are servants" (Lev.
25:55).

(and not servants unto servants) —

yet this man went and got himself a master —

let his ear be pierced.

IN MAN'S POWER

Rabbi Judah bar Simon said in the name of Rabbi Yohanan:

There were three things Moses heard from the Holy One,
blessed be he, and he was taken aback:

When He said to him: "They shall give every man a ransom
   for his soul" (Exod.30:12),
Moses said: Who can give a ransom for his soul?
The Holy One, blessed be he, said to him:
I do not demand of you what is in my power alone,
but that which is in yours.
"This they shall give . . . half a shekel" (Exod.30:13).

It was the same when the Holy One, blessed be he, said to
   Moses:
"Command . . . My food which is presented unto Me for
   offerings made by fire" (Num.28:2).
Moses said: Who can provide Him with offerings enough?
If we were to offer before him all the animals in the field,
and pile up all the trees of the Lebanon,
it would not suffice him.
The Holy One, blessed be he, said to Moses:
I do not demand of you what is in my power alone,
but that which is in yours.
"And thou shalt say unto them: This is the offering made by
   fire . . . he-lambs . . . two day by day. . ." (Num.
   28:3).

It was the same when the Holy One, blessed be he, said to
   Moses:
"And let them make Me a sanctuary, that I may dwell among
   them" (Exod.25:8).
Moses said: Who can make Him a sanctuary, that he shall
   dwell in the midst of it?
"Behold, heaven and the heaven of heavens cannot contain
   Thee" (I Kings 8:27);
"Do not I fill heaven and earth?" (Jer.23:24).

The Holy One, blessed be he, said to Moses:
I do not demand of you what is in my power alone,
but that which is in yours.
If I were to demand it, the whole world could not contain a
    single one of my attendants.
But all I demand of you
is only twenty boards in the south,
and twenty boards in the north,
and eight in the west.

IN THE MIDST OF SORROW

When Moses descended from Mount Sinai, and saw the
    abominations of Israel,
he gazed at the tablets and saw that the words had flown away,
and broke them at the foot of the hill.
At once he fell dumb. He could not say a word.
At that moment a decree was passed concerning Israel,
that they were to study these same words
in the midst of sorrow and in the midst of slavery,
in migration, and in confusion,
in pressing poverty, and in lack of food.
For the sorrow they have suffered,
the Holy One, blessed be he, is destined to reward them dur-
    ing the days of the Messiah,
many times over.

YOU CANNOT FATHOM

"Show me Thy ways, O Lord" (Ps.25:4).
Rabbi Berekhiah said in the name of Rabbi Yohanan:
Like a physician who had a disciple and taught him all the

cures, except the cure for such and such an affliction.

He said to him:

You have revealed to me all the cures in the world except the
cure for such and such an affliction;

I pray you, reveal it to me.

So, Moses said to the Holy One, blessed be he:

"Show me now Thy ways" (Exod.33:13)

— and He "showed" him;

as it is said: "He made known His ways unto Moses" (Ps.
103:7)

— "Show me, I pray thee, Thy glory" (Exod.33:18): Show
me that one of your qualities which is the measure with
which you conduct the world.

He said to him:

You cannot fathom my qualities.

HEAVEN AND MAN

The Holy One, blessed be he, continued to appease Moses.

He said to him:

Am I not your Father, and you my children,

you my brothers, and I your brother;

you my friends, and I your friend;

you my lovers, and I your lover?

Have I allowed you to lack?

All that I ask you is this, as I have examined myself and
found eleven qualities,

so all I ask of you is eleven qualities;

and they are:

"He that walketh uprightly, and worketh righteousness,

And speaketh truth . . ." (Ps.15:2–5).

The Holy One, blessed be he, continued to appease Moses.
He said to him:
Do I at all favor an Israelite or a Gentile,
a man or a woman, a man-servant or a maid-servant?
But whoever he is who keeps a commandment, the reward is
at its heels.
Hence it was said:
He who honors heaven more, heaven's honor is more, and
his own honor is more, as well.
He who honors heaven less, and honors himself more,
heaven's honor continues the same, but his own honor is less.

THE GREAT TREASURE

At that moment He showed Moses all the treasures that are
the reward of each and every one of the righteous for
their deeds.
Moses asked: Whose treasure is this?
He answered: The masters of the Torah.
— And whose treasure is this?
— Those who honor them.
Then He showed Moses a treasure greater than all the rest.
Moses said: Master of the universe, whose is this great treasure?
He said to him:
He who has good deeds, I give him his reward from his own
treasure;
and he who has none of his own, freely I give him from this;
as it is said: "And I will be gracious to whom I will be gra-
cious, and I will show mercy on whom I will show
mercy" (Exod.33:19).

DARING

Levi ordered a public fast, yet no rain came.

He said to God:

Master of the universe, you have gone up and sit on high,
    and you have no compassion on your children.

Then the rain came; but he became lame.

THE INNOCENTS

Hanan the Hidden was the son of the daughter of Honi the
    Circle-Maker.

When the world was in need of rain, the masters would send
    the school children to him,

and they would clutch the hem of his cloak and say to him:

Father, give us rain.

He said to Him:

Master of the universe, do it for the sake of these

who do not know the difference between the Father who
    gives rain and a father who does not give rain.

DEFEAT

"He will not contend for victory" (Ps.103:9).

The Holy One, blessed be he, said:

When I am the victor, I am the loser, and when I am defeated,
    I gain.

I defeated the generation of the Flood

— did I not really lose: for I desolated my world;

as it is written: "And he blotted out every living substance"
    (Gen.7:23).

The same with the generation of the division at the Tower
    of Babel, and the Sodomites.

But in the days of Moses, when I was defeated, I gained, because I did not destroy Israel.

FOR LOVE

Rabbi Yohanan was walking from Tiberias to Sepphoris, and
Rabbi Hiyya bar Abba was supporting him.
They came to a certain field, and Rabbi Yohanan said:
This field was mine, and I sold it in order to gain the Torah.
They came to a certain vineyard, and he said:
This vineyard was mine, and I sold it in order to gain the
Torah.
They came to a certain olive grove, and he said:
This olive grove was mine, and I sold it in order to gain the
Torah.
Rabbi Hiyya began to cry.
Rabbi Yohanan said: Why are you crying?
He said to him: Because you left nothing for your old age.
He said to him: Is what I have done a small thing in your
eyes?
For I have sold a thing which was created in the course of
six days,
and I have gained a thing which was given in the course of
forty days;
as it is said: "And he was there with the Lord forty days and
forty nights" (Exod.34:28).
When Rabbi Yohanan died, his generation read the Writ
over him:
"If a man would give all the substance of his house for love"
— like the love which Rabbi Yohanan had of the Torah —
"would he be contemned?" (Cant.8:7).

"And it came to pass, when Moses came down from mount
   Sinai . . . that Moses knew not that the skin of his face
   sent forth beams" (Exod.34:29).
Whence did Moses get the beams of glory?
Rabbi Judah bar Nehemiah says:
When Moses was writing the Torah, a little was left over in
   his pen, and he passed it over his head,
and that is where he got the beams of glory.

FRAGMENTS

Rabbi Joshua ben Levi said to his sons:
. . . Have care for an old man who has forgotten his learn-
   ing under duress.
For we say:
Tablets and fragments of tablets lie in the Ark of the Cove-
   nant.

COMMENDATION

When Akabia ben Mahalalel was dying, his son said to him:
Father, commend me to some of your comrades.
Akabia said to him:
I will not commend you.
His son said to him: Is it because of some fault you have
   found in me?
He said to him:
No. But your deeds will endear you, and your deeds will
   estrange you.

VIII

A MAN

Rabbi Meir used to say:

Whence do we know that even a Gentile who engages in the
Torah is like a High Priest?

We learn it from: "Ye shall therefore keep My statutes, and
Mine ordinances, which if a man do, he shall live by
them" (Lev.18:5).

"Priests, Levites, and Israelites" was not said,

but "a man";

thus you may learn that even a Gentile who engages in the
Torah

— lo, he is like a High Priest.

A GREATER PRINCIPLE

"Thou shalt love thy neighbour as thyself" (Lev.19:18).

Rabbi Akiba says: This is the great principle of the Torah.

Ben Azzai says: "This is the book of the generations of Adam: In the day that God created man, in the likeness of God made He him" (Gen.5:1) —

this is a principle greater than that.

THE REST IS COMMENTARY

Once a heathen came before Shammai. He said to him:

I will be converted, if you can teach me all the Torah while I stand on one leg.

Shammai pushed him away with the builder's measure he had in his hand.

The man came before Hillel. He converted him.

He said to him:

What is hateful to you, do not do to your fellow.

That is all the Torah. The rest is commentary — go and study.

SICKNESS

"Happy is he that considereth the poor" (Ps.41:2).

Rav Huna said: That is he who visits the sick.

For, Rav Huna said: All who visit the sick lessen his sickness by one sixtieth part.

Objection was raised:

If so, let sixty go up to visit him, and he can return to the market place with them!

Rav Huna said to those who objected:

Sixty — but only if they each love him as they love themselves

Nevertheless — his suffering is eased.

The Holy One, blessed be he, said to Moses:

Tell Israel that it is not that I require offerings —

all the entire world is mine:

the beast you offer up I have created.

And so it is said: "If I were hungry, I would not tell thee"
    (Ps.50:12):

There is no eating and drinking for me.

Rabbi Hiyya bar Abba said:

The creatures I make do not require what is made from them.

Have you ever in all your days heard it said:

Pour wine on this vine, that it may yield much wine,

pour oil on this olive tree that it may yield much oil?

The creatures I make do not require what is made from
    them —

and shall I require the creatures I make?

ACKNOWLEDGING ONE'S LAND

"For thou shalt not go over this Jordan" (Deut.3:27).

Rabbi Levi said:

Moses said to Him:

Master of the universe, the bones of Joseph are entering the
    land,

and shall I not enter the land?

The Holy One, blessed be he, said to him:

He who acknowledged his land is buried in his land,

and he who did not acknowledge his land is not buried in
    his land.

Whence do we know that Joseph acknowledged his land?

His mistress says: "See, he hath brought in a Hebrew unto
    us" (Gen.39:14),

and Joseph did not deny it, but said:

"For indeed I was stolen away out of the land of the Hebrews"
    (Gen.40:15).

Whence do we know that he was buried in his land?

For it is said: "And the bones of Joseph . . . buried they in
    Shechem" (Josh.24:32).

You who have not acknowledged your land are not to be
    buried in your land.

How? The daughters of Jethro say:

"An Egyptian delivered us out of the hand of the shepherds"
    (Exod.2:19),

and he hears it and is silent.

Therefore, he is not to be buried in his land!

"For thou shalt not go over this Jordan."

FIRE OF THE LAW

Ben Azzai was sitting expounding, and a fire shone around
    him.

They came and told Rabbi Akiba:

Rabbi, Ben Azzai is sitting expounding, and a fire is shining
    around him.

He went to Ben Azzai and said to him:

I have heard that you were expounding, and a fire was shin-
    ing around you.

He said: I was, I was.

He said to him: Were you engaged in the mysteries of the
    Divine Throne?

He said to him:

No, but I was sitting and linking the words of the Torah to
    one another and to the Prophets, and the Prophets to
    the Writings,

and the words were as happy as on the day they were given
from Sinai,
and as sweet as at the time they were given.
And were they not given from Sinai in fire?
As it is written: ". . . and the mountain burned with fire"
(Deut.4:11).

IN FAREWELL

When the masters left the house of Rabbi Ammi — some say
it was the house of Rabbi Hanina — they said to him:
May you find your world in your lifetime,
and your future be realized in the life of the world to come,
your hope throughout the generations.
May your heart meditate in understanding,
your mouth speak wisdom,
your tongue move in songs of jubilation,
your eyelids look straight before you,
your eyes be alight with the light of the Torah,
and your face shine with the glow of the firmament;
may your lips utter knowledge,
and your reins rejoice uprightly,
and your footsteps hasten to hear the words of the Ancient
of Days.

FOR EVERY MEASURE

A man must recite a benediction for evil, just as he recites a
benediction for good.
For it is said:
"And thou shalt love the Lord thy God with all thy heart, and
with all thy soul, and with all thy might" (Deut.6:5).

"With all thy heart" — with thy two wills, with thy will to
   good and thy will to evil.
"And with all thy soul" — even if He take thy soul from thee.
"And with all thy might" — for every measure that He meas-
   ures out to thee,
thank him with all thy might.

WITH THY SUBSTANCE

"Honour the Lord with thy substance" (Prov.3:9)
— With the substance he has granted you.
If you have beauty, do not go a-whoring,
but honor your Creator and fear him and praise him for the
   beauty he has given you.
If you have a good voice, and are seated in the House of
   Prayer,
stand and honor the Lord with your voice.
Hiyya, the son of the sister of Rabbi Eliezer ha-Kappar had a
   good voice.
Rabbi Eliezer used to say to him:
Hiyya, my son, stand and honor the Lord with that which he
   has granted you.

THE LORD IS ONE

"And thou shalt love the Lord thy God with all thy heart,
   and with all thy soul . . ." (Deut.6:5).
Rabbi Akiba says: "With all thy soul" — even if He take thy
   soul from thee. . . .
When Rabbi Akiba was taken out to be killed by the Romans,
   it was the time
for the reading of "Hear, O Israel,"

and they kept flaying his flesh with iron combs,

yet he accepted upon himself the yoke of the kingdom of
  heaven.

His disciples said to him:

Still constant, master?

He said to them: All my days I was troubled by this exposi-
  tion:

" 'With all thy soul' — even if He take thy soul from thee."

I said, O that it were in my power to fulfil this!

And now that it is in my power, shall I not fulfil it?

He kept prolonging the "One," until his spirit left him at
  "One."

A voice issued from heaven and said:

Happy are you, Rabbi Akiba, that your spirit has left you at
  "One."

SANCTIFICATION

Rav Pappa said to Abbayi:

How was it that miracles happened to the early masters,

and no miracles happen to us?

Should you say, it is because of their learning;

why in the days of Rav Judah all they studied was the Order
  of Damages,

while we study all the six orders.

Yet, while Rav Judah was simply taking off one shoe before
  prayer, the rains fell;

while we afflict our souls and cry out, and no one heeds us.

He said to him:

The early masters gave their souls for the sanctification of
  the Name of God.

We are not giving our souls for the sanctification of the
  Name of God.

Raba said, and some say, Rav Hisda:

If a man sees chastisements coming upon him, let him search
his deeds.

If he has searched his deeds and found nothing, let him lay
it to his idleness in Torah.

And if he has laid it to that and found nothing,

surely they are chastisements of love.

As it is said: "For whom the Lord loveth He correcteth"
(Prov.3:12).

CHASTISEMENTS

Rabbi Simeon ben Yohai says:

Chastisements are precious;

for the Holy One, blessed be he, gave three gifts to Israel
which the nations of the world desire,

and he gave them to Israel only through chastisements.

They are:

The Torah, and the land of Israel, and the world to come.

Whence do we know this of the Torah?

For it is written: "Happy is the man whom thou chastenest,
O Lord, and teachest him out of thy Torah" (Ps.94:12).

Whence do we know this of the land of Israel?

For it is written: "So the Lord thy God chasteneth thee"
(Deut.8:5),

and afterward: "The Lord thy God bringeth thee into a good
land, a land of brooks of water, of fountains and depths,
springing forth in valleys and hills" (ibid. v.7).

Whence do we know this of the world to come?

For it is written: "For the commandment is a lamp, and the
    teaching is light, and reproofs of instruction are the way
    of life" (Prov.6:23).
Which is the way that brings a man to the world to come?
It is chastisement.

A SMALL THING

Rabbi Hanina said:
All is in the hands of heaven except the fear of heaven.
As it is said: "And now, Israel, what doth the Lord thy God
    require of thee, but to fear the Lord thy God" (Deut.
    10:12).
But is the fear of heaven so small a thing?
And did not Rabbi Hanina say in the name of Rabbi Simeon
    ben Yohai:
All the Holy One, blessed be he, has in his treasure house is
    the treasure of the fear of heaven;
As it is said: "And the fear of the Lord which is His treasure"
    (Isa.33:6).
Yes. For Moses it was a small thing.
As Rabbi Hanina said:
This may be compared to a man who is asked for a large ves-
    sel, and has one, so it seems a small thing to him;
but a small vessel which he has not seems large.

OUT OF LOVE

Should you say:
Lo, I am learning Torah that I may become rich,
and that I may be called "Master,"

and that I may receive a reward

— therefore it is said: "to love the Lord your God" (Deut.
11:13)

— all that you do you must do only out of love.

SURPASSING BOTH

King David said:

I, what am I in this world?

I have been fearful in the midst of my joy, and have rejoiced
in the midst of my fear,

and my love has surpassed them both.

LONGING

"The righteous shall flourish like the palm tree" (Ps.92:13).

As the heart of the palm tree reaches upward,

so the heart of Israel reaches upward to their Father who is
in heaven.

Another interpretation:

As the palm tree has a longing, so the righteous have a longing.

What is their longing?

They long for the Holy One, blessed be he.

Rabbi Tanhuma said:

Once it happened that a certain palm tree standing in Em-
maus bore no fruit;

though they kept engrafting it, still it bore no fruit.

The palm-gardener said to them:

This palm tree sees a palm tree in Jericho and longs for him
with all her heart.

So they brought a sprig from the palm tree in Jericho and
    engrafted it on the palm tree in Emmaus,
and it bore fruit at once.
So it is with the righteous:
All they long and hope for is the Holy One, blessed be he.

MEETING

How does a man find his Father who is in heaven?
He finds him by good deeds, and study of the Torah.
And the Holy One, blessed be he, finds man
through love, through brotherhood, through respect,
through companionship, through truth, through peace,
through bending the knee, through humility,
through studious session, through commerce lessened,
through the service of the masters, through the discussion of
    students,
through a good heart, through decency,
through No that is really No,
through Yes that is really Yes.

THE BEAST

Rav Judah said in the name of Rav:
It is forbidden for a man to eat before having fed his beast.
For it is said: "And I will give grass in the field for thy cattle"
and afterward: "And thou shalt eat and be satisfied" (Deut.
    11:15).

EQUALITY

Should you say:
There are children of the elders,
and there are children of the great,
and there are children of the prophets
— it is said:
"If ye shall diligently keep *all* this commandment" (Deut. 11:22):
the Writ tells us that *all* are equal in the Torah.
And so it is said:
"Moses commanded us a law, an inheritance of the congregation of Jacob" (Deut.33:4).
— "Priests, Levites, and Israelites" is not written here,
but: "the congregation of Jacob."

TO IMITATE GOD

"To walk in all His ways" (Deut.11:22).
Those are the ways of the Holy One, blessed be he;
as it is said: "The Lord, the Lord, God, merciful and gracious, long-suffering and abundant in goodness and truth; keeping mercy unto the thousandth generation, forgiving iniquity and transgression and sin. . ." (Exod.34:6);
and it is said:
"Whoever shall call on the name of the Lord shall be delivered" (Joel 3:5).
But how can a man call on the name of the Lord?
Rather: as the Omnipresent is called merciful and gracious, you too must be merciful and gracious, and give freely to all.
As the Holy One, blessed be he, is called righteous,

as it is said: "The Lord is righteous in all His ways" (Ps.
        145:17),
you too must be righteous.
As the Holy One, blessed be he, is called kindly,
as it is said: "And kindly in all His works" (*ibid.*),
you too must be kindly.

RESIGN THYSELF

Mar Ukba sent to Rabbi Eleazar:
There are men who are against me whom I can deliver into
        the hands of the state.
What shall I do?
Rabbi Eleazar drew lines and wrote:
"I said: 'I will take heed to my ways, that I sin not with my
        tongue;
I will keep a curb upon my mouth, while the wicked is be-
        fore me'" (Ps.39:2):
though the wicked is before me, I will keep a curb upon my
        mouth.
Mar Ukba sent to him again:
They are hard at me, and I cannot bear it.
He sent the message back:
"Resign thyself unto the Lord, and wait patiently for Him"
        (Ps.37:7).

IX

CHILDREN

"Ye are the children of the Lord your God" (Deut.14:1).
When ye act as children should, ye are called children.
When ye do not act as children should, ye are not called chil-
    dren —
the words of Rabbi Judah.
Rabbi Meir says:
In either event ye are called children.

WITH THEE

"Because he [the slave] fareth well with thee" (Deut.15:16)
— With thee in food, with thee in drink.
That thou eat not white bread and he black,
thou drink old wine and he new,
thou sleep on cushions and he sleep on straw.
Hence, they say:
He who gets himself a Hebrew slave
gets himself a master.

The Holy One, blessed be he, said to Israel:

You have four in your household: your son, and your daughter, and your man-servant, and your maid-servant;

and I too have four: the Levite, and the stranger, and the
fatherless, and the widow.

And they are all in one verse:

"And thou shalt rejoice in thy feast, thou, and thy son, and
thy daughter, and thy man-servant, and thy maid-servant,
and the Levite, the stranger, and the fatherless, and the
widow that are within thy gates" (Deut.16:14).

The Holy One, blessed be he, said:

I said that you should make joyful that which is yours and
that which is mine on the holy days which I have given
you.

If you do so, I too will make joyful that which is yours and
that which is mine.

Both the one and the other I am destined to make joyful in
my chosen Temple;

as it is said: "Even them will I bring to My holy mountain,
and make them joyful in My house of prayer" (Isa.56:7).

HOW TO GIVE

Abba bar Ba gave Samuel his son money to divide among the
poor.

He went out and found a poor man eating meat and drinking
wine.

He came and told his father.

Abba said to him:

Give him more, for his soul is bitter.

A RED HALTER

Elijah said to Bar He He, and some say to Rabbi Eleazar:

What is the meaning of the Writ:

"Behold, I have refined thee, but not as silver; I have tried
thee in the furnace of poverty" (Isa.48:10)

— teaching that the Holy One, blessed be he, went over all
the good qualities that he might give Israel, and found
poverty the best.

Samuel said, and some say, Rav Joseph:

That is what people say:

Poverty is becoming to Jews, like a red halter on a white
horse.

MAKING PEACE

See how great is his reward who makes peace between men.

It is written: "Thou shalt build the altar of the Lord thy God
of unhewn stones" (Deut.27:6).

If these stones which cannot hear and cannot see and cannot
smell and cannot speak,

because they make peace between men through the sacrifices
that are offered upon them

the Writ saves them from the sword and declares:

"Thou shalt lift no iron tool upon them" (*ibid.* v.5)

— man, who can hear and see and smell and speak —

how much more is this true of him, when he makes peace
between his fellow men.

EVERY DAY

"Keep silence and hear, O Israel; this day thou art become a
people unto the Lord thy God" (Deut.27:9).

But was the Torah given to Israel on this day?

For this day was at the end of the forty years in the wilderness.

But — this is to teach you that every day the Torah is dear to
those who study it,

as on the day it was given from Mount Sinai.

THE TORCH

Rabbi Yose said:

All my days I was troubled by this verse:

"And thou shalt grope at noonday, as the blind gropeth in
darkness" (Deut.28:29).

What difference (I said) to the blind whether it be darkness
or light?

Until once I happened upon its meaning.

Once I was walking about in the blackness of night and in
darkness, and saw a blind man walking with a torch in
his hand.

I said to him: My son, why the torch?

He said to me: So long as this torch is in my hand, people
see me and save me from the pits and the thorns and the
thistles.

NEAR TO YOU

"For this commandment which I command thee this day, it is
not too hard for thee, neither is it far off. It is not in
heaven. . . . Neither is it beyond the sea . . ." (Deut.
30:11–13).

They said to him:

Moses our master, lo, you say to us it is not in heaven and
it is not beyond the sea.

Then where is it?

He said to them:

In a place that "is very nigh unto thee, in thy mouth, and in
thy heart, that thou mayest do it" (*ibid.* v.14) —

It is not far from you, it is near to you.

·TORAH ON EARTH

. . . On that day Rabbi Eliezer brought all the proofs in the
world, and the masters would not accept them.

He said to them: If the law is according to me, let this locust
tree prove it.

The locust tree moved a hundred cubits. (And some say: four
hundred cubits.)

They said to him: The locust tree cannot prove anything.

Then he said to them: If the law is according to me, let this
stream of water prove it.

The stream of water turned and flowed backward.

They said to him: The stream cannot prove anything.

Then he said to them: If the law is according to me, let the
walls of the House of Study prove it.

The walls of the House of Study began to topple.

Rabbi Joshua reprimanded them:

If scholars are disputing with one another about the law,
what business is it of yours?

They did not fall down out of respect for Rabbi Joshua, and
did not straighten up out of respect for Rabbi Eliezer,
and they are still inclined.

Then he said to them: If the law is according to me, let the
heaven prove it.

A voice came forth from heaven and said:

Why do you dispute with Rabbi Eliezer?

The law is according to him in every case.

Rabbi Joshua rose to his feet and said:

"It is not in heaven" (Deut.30:12).

What is the meaning of: "It is not in heaven"?

Rabbi Jeremiah said:

The Torah has already been given once and for all from
Mount Sinai;

we do not listen to voices from heaven.

For You have already written in the Torah on Mount Sinai:

"After the majority must one incline" (Exod.23:2).

Rabbi Nathan came upon Elijah.

He said to him: What was the Holy One, blessed be he, doing
at that moment?

Elijah said to him:

He was smiling and saying: My children have defeated me,
my children have defeated me!

THE TRAPPER AND THE TORAH

Elijah, of blessed memory, said:

Once I was on a journey and came upon a certain man who
began to mock and scoff at me.

I said to him: What will you answer on the Day of Judgment,
since you have not learned Torah?

He said: I will be able to answer: I was given no understanding and knowledge and intelligence by heaven.

I said to him: What is your trade?

He said to me: I am a trapper of birds and fish.

I said to him:

Who gave you the knowledge and intelligence to take flax
and to spin and to weave it, and to make nets, and to
take fish and birds in them, and to sell them?

He said to me: The understanding and knowledge for that
were given me by heaven.

I said to him: You were given understanding and knowledge
to take the flax, to spin and to weave it, and to take fish
and birds in the nets,

but you were given no understanding to gain Torah?

Yet it is written:

"But the word is very nigh unto thee, in thy mouth, and in
thy heart that thou mayest do it" (Deut.30:14).

At once he considered the matter in his heart, and lifted up
his voice in weeping.

THE WAY OF DEATH

Moses said to the Holy One, blessed be he:

Master of the universe, clear and known to you is the labor
and pain I endured that Israel might come to believe
in your Name.

How much pain I suffered until I established the Torah and
commandments in them.

I said to myself, As I have known their distress, so shall I
know their good days.

And now that the good days of Israel have come, you say to
me:

"Thou shalt not go over this Jordan" (Deut.31:2).

Behold, you are making a fraud of your Torah.

For it is written of the laborer:

"In the same day thou shalt give him his hire, neither shall
the sun go down upon it, for he is poor and setteth his
heart upon it" (Deut.24:15).

Is this the reward for the forty years I have labored that they
might become a holy and faithful people?

He said to him:
"Let it suffice thee" (Deut.3:26).

He said to Him:
Master of the universe, if you will not take me into the land
    of Israel,
let me stay on like the beasts of the field, who eat grass and
    drink water, and live and enjoy the world.
So let my soul be as one of them.
He said to him:
"Let it suffice thee."

He said to Him:
Master of the universe, and if not that,
then let me stay on in this world as a bird that flies to the
    four winds of the earth, and daily gathers its food, and
    returns to its nest at evening.
Let my soul be as one of them.
He said to him:
"Let it suffice thee."

When Moses saw that no creature could save him from the
    way of death,
at that moment he said:
"The Rock, His work is perfect; for all His ways are justice"
    (Deut.32:4).

FIRE

The Torah is called a "fiery law" (Deut.33:2).
Rabbi Yohanan said:
Let all who come to engage in the Torah
see themselves as standing in the midst of fire.

"So Moses the servant of the Lord died there" (Deut.34:5).

Could Moses have been alive and have written, "So Moses
died there"?

But: Till then Moses wrote: from then on Joshua the son of
Nun wrote —

these are the words of Rabbi Judah, and some say of Rabbi
Nehemiah.

Rabbi Simeon said:

Could even a letter be failing in the Torah?

But: Till then the Holy One, blessed be he, spoke, and Moses
repeated what he said, and wrote.

From then on the Holy One, blessed be he, spoke, and Moses
wrote, in tears.

PEACE AFTER TOIL

When Rabbi Judah the Prince lay dying, he pointed his ten
fingers to heaven and said:

Master of the universe, it is clear and known to you

that I have toiled for the Torah with these ten fingers,

and have gotten not one finger's worth of pleasure.

May it be your will that there be peace in my resting place.

A voice issued from heaven and said:

"He entereth into peace,

They rest in their beds" (Isa.57:2).

TO CRY OR TO REJOICE

When a man is born, all rejoice; when a man dies, all cry.

But it should not be so. For when a man is born, one ought
not to rejoice over him, for there is no knowing his fate

and his deeds, whether he will be righteous or wicked,
   good or evil;
and when he dies, one ought to rejoice, for he is departing
   with a good name, and going out of the world in peace.

A LONG SLEEP

A daughter of Rav Hisda said to him:
Does the master desire to sleep a little?
He said to her:
Soon our days will be both long and short,
and we shall sleep long and well.

COMING AND GOING

It has been taught in the name of Rabbi Meir:
When a man comes into the world, his hands are clenched,
as though to say: All the entire world is mine; now I shall
   acquire it.
And when he goes out of the world, his hands are wide open,
as though to say: I have acquired nothing from this world.

EPHEMERA

Samuel said to Rav Judah:
O Keen One, open your mouth and read the Torah, open
   your mouth and learn the law,
that your studies may endure and you may live long.
O Keen One, snatch and eat, snatch and drink,
for the world we must go from is like a wedding feast.

Rav said to Rav Hamnuna:
My son, if you can, favor yourself,

for there is no delight in the netherworld,
and death will not delay.
Men are like the grass in the field:
some growing and some fading.

FINAL JUDGMENT

Raba said:
When a man is led in to be judged, he is asked:
Have you done your business faithfully?
Have you set yourself regular periods to study the Torah?
Have you begotten children after you?
Have you looked forward to redemption?
Have you used all your wits in the study of the law?
Have you understood how one thing will follow from an-
    other?
Yet even so — if "the fear of the Lord is his treasure" (Isa.
    33:6), it will go well with him;
if not, it will not.

X

CAESAREA AND JERUSALEM

Caesarea and Jerusalem:

If a man should tell you they are both in ruins, do not believe it.

That they are both inhabited, do not believe it.

That Caesarea is in ruins and Jerusalem inhabited,

or Jerusalem in ruins and Caesarea inhabited — believe it.

THE RETURN OF THE KEYS

Our masters have taught:

When the Temple was being destroyed for the first time, the young priests assembled in bands with the keys of the Sanctuary in their hands, and went up to the roof of the Sanctuary, and said before Him:

Master of the universe, seeing that we have not been worthy to be faithful treasurers, let the keys be given back to you,

and they threw them heavenwards.

Then something like a hand came forth and received the keys from them.

And they leaped and fell into the fire.

DIVINE PRESENCE IN EXILE

You find:

Every place where Israel was exiled, the Divine Presence was
    with them.

They were exiled to Egypt, the Presence was with them.

They were exiled to Babylon, the Presence was with them.

They were exiled to Elam, the Presence was with them.

They were exiled to Rome, the Presence was with them.

And when they shall return, the Presence, as it were, will be
    with them.

RACHEL WEEPING

Our mother Rachel came forward before the Holy One,
    blessed be he, and said:

Master of the universe, it is clearly known to you

how your servant Jacob loved me with an exceeding love,

and worked seven years for my father for me,

and when he had completed those seven years,

and the time came for my marriage to my husband,

my father took counsel, and gave my sister to my husband in
    my stead.

And it was a very hard thing for me to bear,

yet I had compassion on my sister,

lest she go forth to shame,

and I acted with charity toward her,

and was not jealous of her.

And if I, who am flesh and blood, dust and ashes,

was not jealous of my rival,

and did not send her forth to shame and disgrace,

You, O King, living, enduring, and compassionate,

why are you jealous of idols which are nothing real,
and have exiled my children,
so that they were killed by the sword,
and the foe did with them as they wished?

At once the compassion of the Holy One, blessed be he, was
aroused, and he said:
For your sake, Rachel, I shall return Israel to their place.
Therefore it is written:
"Thus saith the Lord:
A voice is heard in Ramah, lamentation, and bitter weeping,
Rachel weeping for her children;
she refuseth to be comforted for her children, because they
are not" (Jer.31:15).
And it is written:
"Thus saith the Lord:
Refrain thy voice from weeping, and thine eyes from tears;
for thy work shall be rewarded" (*ibid.* v.16).
And it is written:
"And there is hope for thy future
and thy children shall return to their own border" (*ibid.*
v.17).

I SAT ALONE

Rabbi Abba bar Kahana began:
"I sat not in the assembly of them that make merry, nor rejoiced; I sat alone because of thy hand" (Jer.15:17).
The congregation of Israel said to the Holy One, blessed be
he:
Master of the universe, never in all my days have I entered
the theaters and circuses of the nations of the world,

or made merry with them, or rejoiced.

"I sat alone because of thy hand":

The hand of Pharaoh fell upon me, and I did not sit alone.

The hand of Sennacherib fell upon me, and I did not sit
   alone.

But when your hand fell upon me, I sat alone!

FOR LOVE'S SAKE

"For I am love-sick" (Cant.2:5).

The congregation of Israel said to the Holy One, blessed be
   he:

Master of the universe, all the ills you bring upon me —

are to bring me to love you the more.

Another interpretation:

The congregation of Israel said to the Holy One, blessed be
   he:

Master of the universe, all the ills the nations of the world
   bring upon me —

are because I love you.

ROYAL COMMAND AND THAT OF GOD

Rabbi Samuel bar Susreta went up to Rome.

The queen lost a precious ornament and he found it.

A proclamation went out throughout the country:

Whoever returns it in the course of thirty days, will receive
   such and such; after thirty days his head will be cut off.

He did not return it during the thirty days;

after the thirty days he returned it.

She said to him: Were you not in the country?

He said: Yes.

She said to him: And did you not hear the proclamation?

He said: Yes.

She said: And what did it say?

He said to her: Whoever returns it in the course of thirty
days, will receive such and such;

after thirty days, his head will be cut off.

She said to him: Then why did you not return it in the course
of thirty days?

He said to her:

That you might not say I did it out of fear of you,

but rather: out of fear of God.

She said to him:

Blessed be the God of the Jews!

HATE OF JEWS

A Jew passed before Hadrian, and greeted him.

He said to him: What are you? Said he to him: A Jew.

He said to him: Now, shall a Jew pass before Hadrian and
greet him?

And he said: Go and cut his head off.

Another passed and saw what had happened to the first, and
did not greet Hadrian.

He said to him: What are you? Said he to him: A Jew.

He said to him: Now, shall a Jew pass before Hadrian, and
not greet him?

Said he to them: Go and cut his head off.

His councilors said to him: We do not understand why you
have done what you have done. For he who greeted you
is to be killed, and he who did not greet you is to be
killed.

Said he to them: And you want to tell me how to deal with
my enemies?

MARTYRDOM

Once it happened that four hundred boys and girls were
    captured for shameful purposes.

They realized why they were wanted and said:

If we drown in the sea, shall we have the life of the world to
    come?

The eldest of them expounded:

"The Lord said . . . I will bring them back from the depths
    of the sea" (Ps.68:23).

"I will bring them back" — those who drown in the sea.

As soon as the girls heard this, they all leaped into the sea.

The boys argued:

If these, whose nature it is to succumb, do so,

how much more ought we to do so, whose nature it is not to
    succumb.

They too leaped into the sea.

And it is of them that the Writ says:

"For Thy sake are we killed all the day; we are accounted as
    sheep for the slaughter" (Ps.44:23).

SELF-PRESERVATION

Two disciples of Rabbi Joshua changed their coats during a
    time of persecution.

A certain Roman officer met them and said:

If you are the sons of the Torah, give up your lives for its
    sake.

If you are not the sons of the Torah, why be killed for its
    sake?

They said to him:

We are its sons, and are ready to be killed for its sake;

but it is not man's way to destroy himself.

TODAY

Rabbi Joshua ben Levi came upon Elijah standing at the
   entry to the cave of Rabbi Simeon ben Yohai.
He said to Elijah: When will the Messiah come?
He said: Go ask him.
— And where is he to be found?
— At the gates of Rome.
— And what are his signs?
— He is sitting among the beggars suffering from sores. They
   all remove and remake all their bandages at once, but
   he removes and remakes his one at a time, thinking:
   Should I be required, I shall not be delayed.
Rabbi Joshua went there. He said to the Messiah: Peace to
   you, my master and teacher.
He said to him: Peace to you, son of Levi.
He said: When will the master come?
He said: Today.
— Rabbi Joshua went to Elijah and said to him:
He lied to me, for he said he would come today, and he has
   not come.
Elijah said to him: Thus he said to **you:**
"Today — if ye would but hearken to His voice!" (Ps.95:7).

THE SUFFERINGS OF THE MESSIAH

The seven years in which the Messiah, son of David, is to
   come,
iron beams will be brought and laid on his neck, until he is
   stooped,
and he will scream and cry, and his voice will ascend on high.
He will say to Him:
Master of the universe, how long can my strength persist,

how long my spirit, how long my soul, and how long my
limbs?

Am I not flesh and blood?

It was for that moment to come that David wept and said:

"My strength is dried up like a potsherd" (Ps.22:16).

At that moment, the Holy One, blessed be he, will say to
him:

Ephraim, my righteous Messiah,

you have already accepted upon yourself all the suffering
from the six days of Creation.

Now let your sorrow be as my sorrow.

For, from the day wicked Nebuchadnezzar ascended and destroyed my house, and burned my habitation,

and exiled my children among the nations,

by your life and the life of my head,

I have not sat in my throne.

At that moment the Messiah will say to him:

Master of the universe, now I am content.

It is enough for a servant to be like his master.

THE KING IN HIS BEAUTY

The Holy One, blessed be he, is destined to sit in his great
House of Study, and the righteous of the world to sit
before him,

and he to say to them:

My children, it is I for whom you were delivered to death,

it is I for whom you were killed.

You are like me, and I am like you;

as I am living for ever, living and enduring for ever and ever,
so shall you be living and enduring for ever and ever;
as it is said:
"Thine eyes shall see the king in his beauty" (Isa.33:17).

THY KING COMETH

"We will be glad and rejoice in thee" (Cant.1:4).
Like a queen whose husband the king and sons and sons-in-
    law had gone overseas.
Later, messengers came and told her: Your sons have come
    back.
She said: What matter to me? Let my daughters-in-law re-
    joice.
When her sons-in-law came back, they told her: Your sons-
    in-law have come.
She said: What matter to me? Let my daughters rejoice.
They said to her: The king your husband has come.
She said: This is the real delight.

So, in time to come, the prophets will come to Jerusalem and
    say (Isa.60:4):
"Thy sons come from afar,"
and she will say to them: What matter to me?
"And thy daughters are borne on the side";
she will say: What matter to me?
But when they tell her (Zech.9:9):
"Behold, thy king cometh unto thee,
He is triumphant and victorious,"
she will say: This is the real delight;
as it is said: "Rejoice greatly, O daughter of Zion" (*ibid.*).

At that moment she will say (Isa.61:10):
"I will greatly rejoice in the Lord,
My soul shall be joyful in my God."

THE TWO JERUSALEMS

Rabbi Yohanan said:

Not like the Jerusalem of this world is the Jerusalem of the
    world to come.

The Jerusalem of this world: All who wish to ascend to it,
    may ascend.

That of the world to come: They only will enter there who
    are called.

THE REAL REDEMPTION

Israel said to the Holy One, blessed be he:

But have you not redeemed us already by the hands of Moses
    and Joshua and all the judges and kings?

Yet now are we to return to be enslaved and be ashamed, as
    though we had never been redeemed?

The Holy One, blessed be he, said to them:

Seeing that your redemption was at the hands of flesh and
    blood,

and your leaders were men, here today, tomorrow in the
    grave;

therefore your redemption has been redemption for a space.

But in time to come I will redeem you by my own hand;

I, who am living and enduring,

will redeem you with a redemption enduring forever;

as it is said:

"O Israel, that art saved by the Lord with an everlasting
    salvation" (Isa.45:17).

"For with thee is the fountain of life; in Thy light do we see
light" (Ps.36:10).

Rabbi Yohanan said:

As one who was journeying at the time of the sinking of the
sun,

and someone came and lit a candle for him, and it went out;

and another came and lit a candle for him, and it went out.

He said: From now on, I shall wait for the morning light
alone.

So, Israel said to the Holy One, blessed be he:

Master of the universe, we made a lamp for you in the days of
Moses, and it went out;

ten lamps in the days of Solomon, and they went out.

From now on we will wait for your light alone:

"In Thy light do we see light."

CHAPTER ONE

9 In Its Due Time: Gen. Rabbah IX.2.

9 The Grasses Went Forth: Hullin 60b.

10 Harmony: Tanhuma on Gen. 2:4 (Buber, p.11).

11 The Making of Man: Gen. Rabbah VIII.5. — *Man is (already) made:* Heb., *naasah* adam; the allusion is to "Let us make man": Heb., *naaseh* adam. — *Your own seal:* The seal of God is truth.

11 From All the World: Sanhedrin 38a–b.

12 One Pillar: Hagigah 12b. — *foundation of the world:* midrashic interpretation of a phrase originally meaning: an everlasting foundation.

12 Conception: Niddah 16b. — The motive underlying this story is expanded in Seder Yetzirat ha-Velad (Jellinek, Bet ha-Midrash I). — *All is in the hands of heaven:* see Berakhot 33b, based on Deut. 10:12.

13 It Were Better: Erubin 13b. — School of Shammai, school of Hillel: rival schools that arose out of the controversies between Hillel and Shammai (Palestine, 1st cent. B.C.E.–1st cent. C.E.). On the whole Shammai follows a stricter practice, while Hillel is somewhat more lenient. — A "Heavenly Voice" heard in Yavneh decides in favor of the school of Hillel (Erubin 8b; Yerushalmi, Berakhot 3b). — For a historic evaluation of the subject see Louis Ginzberg, Mekomah shel ha-Halakhah be-Toledot Yisrael (1931); and Louis Finkelstein, The Pharisees (1938).

13 Your World: Eccles. Rabbah VII.28. — Pico della Mirandola borrowed this notion for his De hominis dignitate (Rome 1486), a work representative of the spirit of the Renaissance.

13 Singularity: Mishnah Sanhedrin IV.5. — Part of the speech by which the Court impressed the witnesses with the impor-

tance of their testimony. — *a single soul in Israel:* some versions of the Talmud omit "in Israel."

14 The Soul: Lev. Rabbah IV.8.

14 Unique: Seder Eliyahu Rabba II. — *The masters have taught:* Mishnah Sanhedrin IV.5, in discussing why the first man "was created single."

15 If Not for the Will to Evil: First part, Gen. Rabbah IX.9; second part, Yoma 69b. — *will to evil:* Heb., Yetzer ha-Ra; an urge which is opposed to the will to good (Heb., Yetzer ha-Tov). It is not considered as evil per se, but as a power abused by men. It is rather the "passion" in which all human action originates. Man is called upon to serve God "with both wills," directing his passion toward the good and the holy. — *The prophet:* Zechariah.

16 The Iron and the Trees: Gen. Rabbah V.10.

16 Heaven and Earth: Hagigah 12a. — A discussion on the respective preponderance of "heaven" and "earth."

17 The Order of Things: Yoma 38a–b. — *No kingdom touches:* see Berakhot 48b.

CHAPTER TWO

18 Every Day: Seder Eliyahu Rabbah II. — *the Keeper:* trustee. The Midrash (Pesikta Rabbati 74b) calls God "one who keeps in trust all (good deeds) that a man deposits" with him.

18 Ladders: Pesikta de-Rav Kahana 11b–12a. — Compare Luther's answer to the same question: God sits in the primeval forest and cuts whips for people who ask foolish questions.

19 Beauty: Abodah Zarah 20a.

19 Vessels: Taanit 7b.

20 Beauty That Withers: Berakhot 5b. — *Do more, do less:* Menahot 110a. — *two tables:* this world and the world to come. — *my tenth son:* Rabbi Yohanan lost ten sons; he car-

ried a bone (according to the Arukh, a tooth) of the tenth son with him.

21 Grow!: Gen. Rabbah X.7 — *guardian star:* Heb., mazzal; generally, planet. Also, constellation of the zodiac; constellation at one's birth; guardian angel. Cf. Shabbat 156a: "Israel is free from constellational influence."

21 Planting: Lev. Rabbah XXV.3.

21 Greeting the Messiah: Abot de Rabbi Nathan, II.Version, XXXI. — *Rabban Yohanan ben Zakkai:* lived at the time of the destruction of the Second Temple.

21 A Help Meet: Yebamot 63a.

22 Three: Gen. Rabbah XXII.4. — *Divine Presence:* Heb. Shekhinah; divine hypostasis indwelling in the world; Divine Presence among men.

22 Go Down, Go Up: Yebamot 63b.

22 Demands: Erubin 100b.

22 The Generations of Man: Gen. Rabbah XXIV.2. — *its interpreters:* of the law.

23 The Will: Abot de Rabbi Nathan, I.Version, XXXIX. — Compare Rabbi Akiba (Sayings of the Fathers III.19): "Everything is foreseen, yet freedom of choice is given; the world is judged with goodness, yet all is in accordance with the amount of deeds."

CHAPTER THREE

24 The Light That Was Hid: Hagigah 12a. — *The light . . . created on the first day:* in distinction from the sun, the moon and the stars created on the fourth day (Gen. 1:14–19).

24 In Your Power: Tanhuma on Gen. 3:22 (Yelamdenu, p.19f.).

25 The Scales: Kiddushin 40a f. — An important point of doctrine underlying the yearly Day of Judgment.

26 Subdual: Midrash Tehillim on 36:7 (Buber, p.250).

26 Man's Deeds: Seder Eliyahu Rabbah IX.

27 Nevertheless: Baba Kamma 50a. — *for pilgrims:* who "went up" to Jerusalem on the three festivals, Passover, Feast of Weeks, and Feast of Booths. — *Hanina ben Dosa:* a man distinguished by his piety and his miraculous deeds; see In Time and Eternity (New York 1946), pp.55–58.

27 Luck: Moed Katan 28a.

28 Retribution: Sayings of the Fathers II.7.

28 The Bitter Olive: Cant. Rabbah IV.2.

28 The Vineyard: Tanhuma on Gen. 9:20 (Yelamdenu, p.42).

29 I Am the Master: Gen. Rabbah XXXIX.1. — The Midrash emphasizes Abraham's own search for the knowledge of God; he was not guided "by a father or a teacher" (Gen. Rabbah LXI.1). On Abraham's spiritual development: Maimonides, Mishneh Torah, Hilkhot Akum I.3.

30 Abraham's Choice: Gen. Rabbah XXXIX.10. — *Aram Naharaim and Aram Nahor:* Mesopotamia. — *Ladder of Tyre:* Scala Tyriorium of the ancients; a promontory south of Tyre from where the land of Canaan could be beheld.

30 As Dust: Gen. Rabbah XLI.12.

31 Seed: Yebamot 64a.

31 World and Justice: Gen. Rabbah XXXIX.6.

32 No Distinction: Baba Kamma 60a.

32 Moment of Judgment: Rosh ha-Shanah 16b; Gen. Rabbah LIII.19. — Ishmael is considered the progenitor of Arab tribes. In the Koran, Ishmael appears as a prophet. — *whose children are destined:* see Lam. Rabbah II.5.

33 The Voice and the Hands: Pesikta de-Rav Kahana 121a. — *Abnimos the weaver* (Heb., ha-gardi): Oinomaos of Gadara (2nd cent.), a member of the philosophical school of the

younger Cynics. Lam. Rabbah Introd. 2 calls Oinomaos and Balaam *the* philosophers of the pagans. — *not "the hands of Esau.":* the hands are without power.

34 Jacob's Ladder: Pesikta de-Rav Kahana 151; Lev. Rabbah XXIX.2. — This midrash attributed to Rabbi Meir (2nd cent.) is a significant example of talmudic reflection on Israel's position in history.

35 The Image in the Window: Sotah 36b. — *ephod:* an outer garment worn by the high priest; on two onyx stones, affixed to the shoulder pieces of the ephod, were engraved the names of the twelve tribes (Exod. 28:6–12; Yoma 71bf.).

CHAPTER FOUR

36 Thornbush: Exod. Rabbah II.9. — *fence of the world:* guarding, protecting the world.

36 Signs: Yebamot 79a.

37 As Oil: Cant. Rabbah I.21.

37 Crossing the River: Yerushalmi, Demai 22a.

38 Community: Taanit 11a.

38 Sharing: Deut. Rabbah II.14.

38 The Yoke of Freedom: Sifre on Deut. 32:39 (Friedmann, 138b).

39 Hearken: Mekhilta on 15:26 (Friedmann, 46a).

39 Sustenance: Mekhilta on 16:14 (Friedmann, 47b).

40 Before You: Mekhilta on 17:6 (Friedmann, 52b).

40 For All to See: Mekhilta on 19:2 (Friedmann, 62a)

40 The Way of Fire: Mekhilta on 19:18 (Friedmann, 65a).

40 All at One Time: Tanhuma on Exod. 20:1 (Yelamdenu, p.249).

41 The Voice: Exod. Rabbah XXIX.9.

41 To Me the Word: Pesikta de-Rav Kahana 110a.

42 Two Views: Hagigah 13b. — The midrash refers to the difference between the elaborate description of the theophany by Ezekiel (Ezek. 1) and the short account by Isaiah (Isa. 6:1–4). A countryman, unaccustomed to see royalty, relates all the details; a townsman can be brief.

42 Guarantors: Cant. Rabbah I.24. *"Whereby shall I know":* the midrash finds fault with Abraham for asking a confirming sign that he is to inherit the land of Canaan. — *"My way is hid":* these words spoken by Jacob *qua* the people of Israel, are ascribed by the midrash to Jacob the patriarch.

43 Tear Down: Megillah 31b.

43 Not Meant for Angels: Shabbat 88b. — *nine hundred* and *seventy-four generations:* the midrash reads Ps. 105:8 to mean: the word He hath commanded to the thousandth generation. Since Moses was of the 26th generation after Adam, the Torah was "hidden" 974 generations before the Creation.

45 The Journey: Hagigah 5a. — *saints:* the perfect ones will not stand the tribulations of a journey through life; the less perfect will mature during the journey.

45 The Nations Refuse the Torah: Sifre on Deut. 33:2 (Friedmann, 142b). — *seven commandments . . . of Noah:* rabbinic conception of basic laws to be accepted by the descendants of Noah, i.e. by all men. They are: prohibition against idolatry, incest, murder, profanation of the name of God, robbery; duty to form instruments of justice; prohibition against eating parts cut from living animals (Sanhedrin 56a f.). Compare Nathan Isaacs, "The Influences of Judaism on Western Law," in The Legacy of Israel (Oxford 1928), p.383ff. Hugo Grotius (17th cent.) took the Noahide commandments as the foundation for his "natural law."

46 Indifferent Love: Seder Eliyahu Rabbah VII.

47 The Gates: Exod. Rabbah XIX.4. — ". . . *to the wanderer":* usual translation: to the roadside.

CHAPTER FIVE

48 Witnesses: Pesikta de-Rav Kahana 102b. — *Simeon ben Yohai:* to this 2nd-cent. talmudic master and severe critic of Rome (Shabbat 33b) popular tradition attributed the authorship of the Zohar, foremost work of Jewish mysticism.

48 Where Is the Torah: Shabbat 89a.

50 Preparation: Seder Eliyahu Rabbah VI.

50 Imitation: Sotah 5a. — *Mount Sinai:* a small mountain.

50 Humility: Seder Eliyahu Rabbah XXVI.

51 Three Things: Moed Katan 28a.

51 Thy Words Be Few: Berakhot 60bf.

51 Not Together: Sotah 5a. — Cf. the hasidic saying: "There is no room for God in him who is full of himself" (M. Buber, Ten Rungs [New York 1947], p.102).

52 Man's Hour: Erubin 13b.

52 As the Desert: Pesikta de-Rav Kahana 107a.

52 As Wine: Sifre on Deut. 11:22 (Friedmann, 84a).

53 Learning: Taanit 7a.

53 Man's Limits: Megillah 6b.

54 He and I: Berakhot 17a. — *Yavneh:* seat of an academy founded by Yohanan ben Zakkai at the time of the destruction of the Second Temple (70 C.E.); Yavneh took the place of Jerusalem in many respects. It was destroyed during the rebellion of Bar Kokhba (132–135). — *"Do more, do less . . .":* Menahot 110a.

54 The Watchmen: Pesikta de-Rav Kahana 120b.

55 Saving the Torah: Baba Metzia 85b.

55 The Oral Law: Seder Eliyahu Zutta II. — *Oral Law:* Heb., Torah shebeal Peh, the originally unwritten tradition which

constitutes the basis of Talmud and Midrash. According to the sages, both the *Written Law* (Torah shebikhtav) and the Oral Law are the divine revelation; this belief was not shared by the Sadducees and the Karaites.

57 The Law and More: Baba Metzia 83a. — *He took away their cloaks:* according to the letter of the talmudic law the negligent worker is responsible for the loss.

57 Stand Up: Makkot 22a.

57 The Ways of Life: Berakhot 28b.

58 As a Dog or Crow: Baba Batra 8a. — *Mishnah . . . Gemara:* parts of the Talmud. — *Halakhah:* law. — *Haggadah* (or, Aggadah): the non-legal homiletical exegesis of the Scriptures. — *ignoramus:* Heb., Am ha-Aretz, literally, the people of the land; in the Talmud it denotes a person who does not study the law and does not live according to the commandments as interpreted by the sages (see Berakhot 47b). "An Am ha-Aretz cannot be pious" (Sayings of the Fathers II.6).

59 Core: Berakhot 63a.

59 David's Harp: Pesikta de-Rav Kahana 62b.

60 Paths: Yerushalmi, Hagigah 77a.

CHAPTER SIX

61 Fathers and Children: Lev. Rabbah XIX.20. — *Hezekiah . . . Ahaz . . . Josiah . . . Amon:* kings of Judah (8th–7th cent. B.C.E.).

62 Four Answers: Pesikta de-Rav Kahana 158a. — *turn in repentance:* Heb., Teshuvah, man's "turning" from his aberrations to the "way of God."

62 The Broken Vessel: Midrash ha-Gadol on Gen. 38:1 (Schechter, p.567).

63 Labor: Abot de Rabbi Nathan, II.Version, XXI.

63 Advice: Pesahim 113a.

64 Sustenance: Mishnah Kiddushin IV.14.

64 Provision: Seder Eliyahu Rabbah XV.

65 Equal in Honor: Seder Eliyahu Rabbah XXIV.

65 Ransom: Horayot 13a.

65 Blood: Pesahim 25b.

65 Altar and Iron: Mekhilta on 20:25 (Friedmann, 74a).

66 Jesters: Taanit 22a. — *Be Hozae:* Khuzistan, a province in southwest Persia. — *Be Lapat:* capital of Khuzistan during the Sasanian period. — *Elijah:* after his ascent to heaven, this prophet, according to legend, continued to appear as a messenger of God, in order to instruct, advise, and befriend the pious. On Elijah in rabbinical literature, see Jewish Encyclopedia V, 122ff.

66 The Guardian of Chastity: Yerushalmi, Taanit 64b.

67 They That Love Him: Shabbat 88b.

CHAPTER SEVEN

68 Principles and Details: Sifre on Deut. 32:2 (Friedmann, 132a).

68 The One Commandment: Makkot 23b f. — *in all the Torah:* by observing all the commandments of the Torah.

70 The Choice: Cant. Rabbah I.9. "The fable of Solomon's Choice is a parable of the history of the Chosen People. . . . They had not sought after those things which the Gentiles seek, but had sought first the kingdom of God; and therefore all those things were added unto them. . . . As for long life, the Jews live on — the same peculiar people — today, long after the Phoenicians and the Philistines have lost their identity like all the nations. The ancient Syriac neighbors of Israel have fallen into the melting-pot and have been reminted, in the fullness of time, with new images and super-

scriptions, while Israel has proved impervious to the alchemy — performed by history in the crucibles of universal states and universal churches and wanderings of the nations — to which we Gentiles all in turn succumb." (Arnold J. Toynbee, A Study of History [London 1935] II,55.)

71 The Ear: Kiddushin 22b. — *This ear heard:* note the version in Yerushalmi, Kiddushin 59d: "This ear heard from Mount Sinai: 'Thou shalt have no other gods before Me' (Exod. 20:3), and cast off the yoke of the Kingdom of heaven and accepted the yoke of flesh and blood . . ."

71 In Man's Power: Lev. Rabbah XII.3. — *twenty boards:* for the tabernacle in the wilderness (Exod. 26:15–30).

73 In the Midst of Sorrow: Seder Eliyahu Rabbah XIX. — *abominations:* the golden calf.

73 You Cannot Fathom: Midrash Tehillim on 25:4 (Buber, p.211).

74 Heaven and Man: Seder Eliyahu Rabbah XIV.

75 The Great Treasure: Tanhuma on Exod. 33:19 (Yelamdenu, p.323).

76 Daring: Taanit 25a.

76 The Innocents: Taanit 23b. — *Honi the Circle-Maker:* or, Circle-Drawer (Honi ha-Meaggel), lived around 100 B.C.E. in Jerusalem; noted for his effective prayer.

76 Defeat: Pesikta Rabbati 32b f.; Midrash Tehillim on 103:9 (Buber, p.436). — ". . . *for victory":* usual translation, for ever; Heb., la-Netzah, which can be taken to mean: for victory.

77 For Love: Lev. Rabbah XXX.1.

78 Beams of Glory: Tanhuma on Exod. 34:29 (Buber, p.119). — Compare the reason given in Seder Eliyahu Rabbah IV: "Because he did desire of the Holy One, blessed be he, and was concerned for the honor of the Holy One, blessed be he, and for the honor of Israel all of his days, and yearned and longed and strove to make peace between Israel and their Father who is in heaven."·

78 Fragments: Berakhot 8b.

78 Commendation: Mishnah Eduyot V.7.

CHAPTER EIGHT

79 A Man: Abodah Zarah 3a.

80 A Greater Principle: Sifra on 19:18 (Weiss, 89b).

80 The Rest Is Commentary: Shabbat 31a. — *What is hateful to you:* cf. Tob. 4:15: "What thou thyself hatest, do to no man." On the subject: G. Brockwell King, "The Negative Golden Rule," in The Journal of Religion, VIII (1928), No.2.

80 Sickness: Lev. Rabbah XXXIV.1.

81 Sufficiency: Num. Rabbah XXI.16.

81 Acknowledging One's Land: Deut. Rabbah II.5.

82 Fire of the Law: Cant. Rabbah I.52. — *mysteries of the Divine Throne:* Heb., Merkavah, one of the central themes of the early Kabbalah, based on Ezek. 1, and aiming at a mystical vision of God's throne "which embodies and exemplifies all forms of creation" (G. Scholem, Major Trends in Jewish Mysticism [New York 1946] p.44).

83 In Farewell: Berakhot 17a. — *look straight before you:* in the understanding of the Torah. — *Ancient of Days:* Dan. 7:9.

83 For Every Measure: Mishnah Berakhot IX.5.

84 With Thy Substance: Pesikta Rabbati 127a.

84 The Lord Is One: Berakhot 61b. — *by the Romans:* during the persecutions which followed the breakdown of the Bar Kokhba rebellion in 135 c.e. On the subject: Louis Finkelstein, "The Ten Martyrs," in Essays and Studies in Memory of Linda R. Miller (New York 1938) p.29ff.

85 Sanctification: Berakhot 20a. — *six orders:* sections of the Mishnah.

104 Rachel Weeping: Lam. Rabbah, Proem. XXIV (Buber, p.28).

105 I Sat Alone: Lam. Rabbah, Proem. III (Buber, p.5).

106 For Love's Sake: Cant. Rabbah II.14.

106 Royal Command and That of God: Yerushalmi, Baba Metzia 8c.

107 Hate of Jews: Lam. Rabbah III.41.

108 Martyrdom: Gittin 57b.

108 Self-Preservation: Gen. Rabbah LXXXII.9.

109 Today: Sanhedrin 98a.

109 The Sufferings of the Messiah: Pesikta Rabbati 162a. — *Ephraim:* a name for the Messiah (see Jer. 31:9,20).

110 The King in His Beauty: Seder Eliyahu Rabbah XIV.

111 Thy King Cometh: Cant. Rabbah I.31.

112 The Two Jerusalems: Baba Batra 75b.

112 The Real Redemption: Midrash Tehillim on 31:2 (Buber, p.237).

113 Waiting: Pesikta de-Rav Kahana 144a.